Country Fair

By the same author

Country Fair

Tales of the Countryside, Shooting and Fishing

MAX HASTINGS

Line drawings by
WILLIAM GELDART

HarperCollins*Publishers*

HarperCollins*Publishers*
77–85 Fulham Palace Road,
Hammersmith, London W6 8JB
www.harpercollins.co.uk

Published by HarperCollins*Publishers* 2005

1

The author asserts the moral right to be
identified as the author of this work

A catalogue record for this book is
available from the British Library

ISBN 0 00 719886 8

Set in Granjon by Rowland Phototypesetting Ltd,
Bury St Edmunds, Suffolk

Printed and bound in Great Britain by
Clays Ltd, St Ives plc

For Nigel and Anna,
with whom I have shared so many
happy sporting memories over forty years

Contents

Country Fair

Introduction

*I*N THE EYES of most people likely to read this book, as well as in my own, the countryside is fundamental to the vision of the Britain which we love, and to which we bear allegiance. This is why we find it so distressing today to be ruled by a government which not only cares nothing for the rural community, but has shown itself contemptuously hostile to it. The countryside and its inhabitants are perceived by New Labour as anachronisms, reflecting traditions of patrician paternalism, plebeian deference and bloody pastimes which have no place in the pavement society Tony Blair and his party aspire to enforce. While Labour claims to have abandoned the old ideals of

1

socialism, it displays a disdain for rights of private ownership of a single commodity – land – which would be
deemed intolerably socialistic if applied to any other form
of property. New duties of care are thrust upon landowners, even as a host of new rights of access are granted
to the public. The government proposes a programme of
housing development which, if it is fulfilled, will carpet
in concrete great tracts of fields and woodland, poisoning
the green lungs of this overcrowded island, and especially
its south-eastern corner. Foremost among the aspirations
of rural dwellers today is a desire to see those who rule
us once again acknowledge the virtue and importance of
Britain's countryside to our society, not as a mere park in
which the urban population can seek recreation at
appointed hours on licence, but as a place where wilderness sustains its historic freedoms, not least those of the
hunter, both animal and human.

This book is intended to serve two purposes: first, like
my earlier country collections, to entertain rural sportsmen with tales of the pleasures which we share, embracing fields and streams, dogs and guns, rods and horses.
Second, at a time when the traditional rural community
feels imperilled as never before, I have included essays on
two critical issues: the struggle to sustain our landscape,
and the tensions between English and Scots, a source of
concern to all of us for whom the Union of the two
kingdoms means so much. I hope that these more sombre
pieces will not jar on readers to whom I am otherwise
seeking to offer a little bedside amusement.

Even in these troubled times for rural Britain, I cherish
a spirit of optimism, inspired by the happiness which so

many of us still gain from the countryside. One of my favourite pastimes, while casting a fly or waiting for a drive to begin, is to muse upon the same experiences in the days of our ancestors. A sense of continuity, of doing things which they did, in the old settings, is one of the deepest satisfactions of field sports. As they look down upon our doings with horse, rod and gun, how pampered they must think us! First, mobility offers free rein. We think nothing of driving from London to Wiltshire or Hampshire for a few hours' fishing. I set out from Berkshire the other day to shoot in Devon, and came home easily enough the same evening. I am untroubled by driving to Wales to throw a line, then returning to sleep in my own bed. We can journey to Sutherland – or for that matter, to Russia or Iceland – inside a day.

We pay a price, in that some of the thrilling remoteness has gone from these places. So, too, has the intimacy which attached to a shooting party when guns, beaters and pickers-up lived within a few miles of the meeting place. Everybody knew each other, and the coverts. Today, one often meets a picker-up who has come from thirty miles away, or beaters who travel regularly from distant towns. Shooting and fishing parties forge their own sense of community, but this is seldom now rooted in local geography.

We are much better equipped to face the elements than earlier generations. My father shot in a tailor-made tweed jacket cut loose at the elbows. Waterproof it was not, any more than were his canvas Newmarket boots. Today, conditions must be very damp indeed for water to penetrate to the places where it made our grandparents so uncomfortable. Guns have not changed at all – indeed, many of us shoot with weapons built almost a hundred years ago. As a child, I enjoyed watching my father performing alchemist's rites with powder and shot as he loaded his own cartridges. I occasionally experimented with the process myself, much to the alarm of anyone who later found my overcharged rounds in his gun. But it would be hard to argue that sporting life is poorer now that everybody fires factory-loaded ammunition. When did you last see someone having to use a cartridge extractor?

Fishing rods are wonderfully improved. One would have to be very sentimental to prefer an old greenheart to a new Sage. I am no longer even convinced that old reels are better: I would rather play a modern salmon on a modern reel. Of my father's old tackle, I use only a couple of cane brook rods on chalk streams. Thank heaven fishermen no longer have to grease silk lines or dry gut casts at the end of a day!

Edwardian shooting parties provided opportunities for an orgy of adultery, facilitated by the fact that in large Norfolk or Yorkshire country houses, husbands and wives occupied separate bedrooms. Nowadays, when most of us inhabit more modest quarters, it requires considerable ingenuity for a couple bent on infidelity to find space to swing a cat, never mind themselves, amid a houseful of visiting guns. A friend once told me that a billiard table provided the most discreet rendezvous that she and her weekend quarry could commandeer for naughtiness. Edward VII would have been proud of her. A big shot like Sir Ralph Payne-Galway would have deplored her bloke's frivolous attitude to more serious purposes.

My father sought to convince me that only activities in which one engages actively and individually – notably hunting, shooting and fishing – can properly be described as sports. Soccer and rugger, he suggested dismissively, are mere games. Most of those who call themselves 'sports enthusiasts' are content to spectate, usually from an armchair at home. The old boy has lost that argument, I am afraid. Games reign supreme in public esteem, however dismaying the behaviour of some of those who play them.

The saddest change since father's era is the fungus-growth of hostility towards traditional sports. The other day, I was driving a car full of guns along a bridlepath on the Berkshire Downs. Our convoy was careful to slow and steer aside from ramblers we met. I tried 'Good mornings' out of the window to each of them, but was rewarded only by stony stares. They had seen and heard us banging away, and did not like it. The sight of a pheasant falling wounded or dead from the sky is repugnant to many such rural visitors. It seems sensible to spare their sensitivities by seeking to shoot discreetly. It is no longer a good idea to run drives within sight of a public road.

The banning of fox-hunting signals a threat to the future of all English field sports, as well as a body-blow to the historic life of the countryside. For centuries, hunts have provided a focus for the social lives of many rural communities. At a stroke, and with malice aforethought, the great tradition reflected in the art of Stubbs, Alken and a thousand lesser brushes, and by the pens of Trollope, Surtees, White-Melville, Siegfried Sassoon, has been swept

5

away. Now that Parliament has established the principle that it is wrong to kill one species of wildlife for pleasure, there is no logical reason why politicians should not move against shooting and fishing also.

I am not optimistic about the prospects for sustained defiance of the hunting ban. Those against whom it is directed are instinctively law-abiding people, even if they are now also angry ones. Some symbolic meets will continue for a time. Drag-hunting may prosper. Essentially, however, fox-hunting and legal hare-coursing – the Labour Party is indifferent to illegal coursing by travellers, which raises no class-war blood-lust on its Commons benches – will atrophy. Many of us whose own lives are not directly affected feel a surge of sorrow for what this measure says about the society to which we belong, in which *halal* butchery remains acceptable and the use of soft drugs is tolerated, but testing horses, riders and hounds in pursuit of a fox is not. The hunting ban is the act of an urban dictatorship, intolerant of minority cultures which exist outside parameters determined by itself.

There is nothing new about the contempt of intellectuals and radicals for rural pastimes. Joseph Addison remarked scornfully almost three centuries ago: 'Hunting is not a proper employment for a thinking man.' The unwelcome twenty-first-century novelty is the determination of an urban-based ruling political class to regard a belief in its own moral superiority as sufficient mandate to persecute a rural minority which it despises. It cares nothing for the wise observation of Plato a couple of millennia ago: 'There can be no more important kind of information than the exact knowledge of a man's own country; and for this as well as for more general reasons of pleasure and advantage, hunting with hounds and other kinds of sport should be pursued by the young.' The hunting ban is the act of a government set upon creating a new Britain in its own image, confident that it faces no political opposition strong enough to frustrate its purposes.

We become a drearier and less diverse society with the loss of the pageantry of English fox-hunting, its thrusters and eccentrics, its beaux and belles, its happy meets and silly squabbles. The challenge now, for those who cherish the traditional countryside, is to do everything in our power to ensure that sport with horse and hounds is not altogether lost, and that the other great rural pastimes continue to prosper. The government assures us that it has no intention of legislating against shooting and fishing. We would be rash to swallow such bromides from an administration which has shown itself chronically deceitful on a host of other issues. I have often written about the importance of supporting the countryside organisations, both those which are responsible for sport – the Countryside Alliance, the British Association for Shooting and Conservation, the Game Conservancy – and those which fight for our rural landscape and character, notably the Campaign to Protect Rural England. Today, when so much is at risk, this seems more important than ever. Sceptics shrug: 'What's the point? Nobody has been able

to stop the hunting ban, and nobody can stop this government attacking shooting, or building millions more houses
on green fields.' Yet, just as no thoughtful countryman
regrets the struggle to save fox-hunting, which delayed
legislation for years, so we cannot now succumb to defeat-
ism about shooting, fishing and uncontrolled housing
development. If we do not fight, then our sports and our
landscape do not deserve to survive.

We must make strategy in the consciousness that we
might be ruled by Labour governments for a decade. Tony
Blair's party thinks so, too. Political arrogance fortified
Labour's enthusiasm for banning fox-hunting. It imbues
the party's MPs with a dangerous boldness about the
possibilities for going further in their crusade 'irreversibly
to change the nature of British society'. On our side, in
seeking to resist new encroachments, we should fight a
non-party battle, on an environmental and libertarian
platform. Economic arguments about jobs and rural
income at stake butter few parsnips with our opponents,
for the numbers are too small.

If field sports ally themselves explicitly with the Tories
then, bluntly, we anchor ourselves to a party which cannot
for the foreseeable future offer useful aid. We face a
cultural issue, which extends far beyond field sports.
Britain is changing. Those of us who live familiar rural
lives amid our rose gardens and the routine of planting
broad beans, casting a fly for trout, pursuing grouse,
decoying pigeons, should perceive that we inhabit a precious yet increasingly isolated social capsule. It is magnificent, but in the eyes of many of our fellow-countrymen,
it represents a charade rather than reality. Out there

beyond the gate, there is another world far removed from ours, and politically much more powerful. It is only necessary to ride on a London tube and glance at one's neighbours in the carriage to perceive its nature. Many inhabitants of New Britain and Young Britain possess no interest in studying Old Britain's history or in perpetuating its culture. From our viewpoint, it is futile to waste time lamenting this state of affairs. If we want our fragment of society to survive, we must achieve an accommodation with this new world, which is mistrustful of old elites, inherently sceptical of old values.

A while back, a *Field* reader who proudly described himself as a 'toff' accused me of inverted snobbery. Yet it seems only common sense to recognise that the people banning fox-hunting are motivated chiefly by a commitment to class warfare, not animal welfare. One Labour minister has acknowledged explicitly that the measure represented, in the eyes of himself and his comrades on the Commons benches, 'revenge for the miners'. Tony Blair and his successors may only be dissuaded from further assaults on field sports if they perceive that such action would antagonise those whom they classify as 'ordinary people', rather than merely an old 'privileged class' whom it delights them to punish.

The most admirable quality in politics, as in life, is generosity of spirit. What was done in the House of Commons in 2004 represented a great meanness. Henceforward, to paraphrase Hugh Gaitskell in a somewhat different context: we must fight, fight and fight again to save the way of life we love. We can succeed only by representing this as a battle for social liberty and for the rural environment, not by positioning ourselves behind a conservative or Conservative barricade.

Our forefathers would have recoiled, of course, from the necessity of justifying to the urban population the chosen activities of the rural community. They regarded the pursuit of wild quarry as the most natural of human activities, and they were right. Yet they might also be cheered that in the twenty-first century we are still doing many things which they did, in a manner not so different from that which they knew. Politics casts its sorry shadow, yet politics seems a wonderfully long way away on a June day at a trout lake, or on a fine December morning, when one hears beaters tapping through the wood and the first cock exploding with a clatter from the trees. The past may have seemed less complicated than the present, but our own sporting experience retains an enchantment that would cheer the shades of our ancestors.

This is the third collection of rural writings I have published. I should acknowledge a debt to Robert Lacey, my editor at HarperCollins, who does so much to smooth the eccentricities of my prose, even when these concern implausible nuances of field sports. Much of the book is adapted from pieces I have written over recent years for *The Field*, to whose editor Jonathan Young I owe much. He has become a cherished friend as well as one of Britain's staunchest and shrewdest standard-bearers for the cause of the countryside. I have also included here a chapter based on speeches I have made on behalf of the Campaign to Protect Rural England, concerning the other great countryside issues – the preservation of our green spaces and the way of life of those who inhabit them. The CPRE is strictly neutral on field sports. I should stress that the views expressed in this book are personal, and do not represent those of that body, whose business and membership are fighting for our landscape. The CPRE rightly avoids engagement in such contentious matters as fox-hunting. But preserving our countryside is a challenge embracing many strands. Even if different country people fight different battles, these should be perceived as complementary, not contradictory.

I hope readers will gain pleasure from sharing some of my experiences of rural and sporting life, even if almost all of you are more skilful in their practice than myself. In describing my own doings, the only concession I make to discretion is sometimes to change the names of characters with whom I have shared them, to spare their blushes, if not my own. I am conscious that these writings reflect a privileged experience. In recent years, I have been lucky enough to visit some of the finest rivers and shoots in Britain and abroad, and to enjoy wonderful sporting opportunities. It was not always so. I spent my early sporting life, as most of us do, picking crumbs from beneath the table. My natural habitats for many years were modest day-ticket fisheries and walked-up hedges. I reached great grouse moors and salmon pools only relatively late in the day. I have fed from the silver spoon only after a long acquaintance with a wooden one, which I hope is some excuse for extolling the joys of butts and double-gun days.

I have called this collection *Country Fair*, which reflects the range of joys and beauties we encounter in pursuing our romance with rural Britain. The title also represents a gesture of filial affection, as my first chapter will explain.

Max Hastings
Il Pinquan, Kenya
March 2005

1

Country Fair

*A*s ANYONE WHO reads my writings will have noticed over the years, I am addicted to rural history. Not to nostalgia, because we should recognise that, in the countryside as elsewhere, over the last half-century some things have grown better rather than worse. There is no surer shortcut to senility than forever to be lamenting a lost past. Yet it is always pleasing to relate the world we know today to that which our parents and grandparents inhabited. I have been thumbing through the bound volumes of a now-forgotten magazine named *Country Fair*, which flourished for a time in the 1950s, half a century ago. It holds a special charm for me, because my father created and edited it alongside that great Wiltshire farmer and writer A.G. Street.

Successive issues of *Country Fair* captured snapshots of a world I can just remember, in which the combine harvester was slowly replacing the binder and thresher; BSA advertised a single-barrel shotgun ('hitherto for export only') at £18.2s.11d; and 'B.B.' in his shooting column urged the merits of a stuffed cat as a surefire lure for carrion

13

crows. J. Hughes-Parry described how he gaffed a thirty-seven-pound spring salmon for his wife Pat on the Welsh Dee on 26 March, among a host of lesser monsters which fell to his rod that season. Jack Ivester-Lloyd wrote about hunting clothes, telling me something I never knew: 'The custom observed by many hunts of asking farmers who come out with them to wear black coats and hunting caps came into being for a very good reason. It is done so that others may easily recognise the men over whose land they may be riding and who, therefore, should be treated with special courtesy.' Arthur Street described, with copious diagrams, the art of setting a course to plough a field.

My mother, Anne Scott-James, wrote deploring the fashion in which old cottages in our villages were being pulled down. Landlords found this cheaper than making repairs, when statutory controls restricted many rents to three or four shillings a week. Mother's rage was inspired by the demolition of a very old thatched cottage immediately opposite our own. 'The Whitehall bureaucrats say people must be cleared out of sub-standard properties,' she wrote, 'and they declaim violently against "country slums". They regard a man with money to spend on converting an old cottage with hatred, and talk of "the wrong people" getting homes ... As fast as new houses are built in the country, old ones are pulled down. It doesn't make sense.'

The magazine's 'topic of the month' for July 1951 was that of farm holidays. Agriculture needed a lot of scarce seasonal labour between July and November – 'It wants twelve to reap what it takes one man to sow.' For several decades in the early and mid-twentieth century, townsmen were encouraged to take cheap holidays by boarding or camping on a farm. In high summer they paid thirty-five shillings a week for their keep – £1.75 in modern money – and could earn one shilling and sixpence an hour – around 7p – for their labour. By October and November, the rate for a week's bed and rations on a farm had fallen to a pound, and wages had risen to one shilling and ninepence.

Ralph Wightman, a Dorset farmer who was also a well-known writer of the period, urged the virtues of the farm camper not only to provide a hand, 'but because his labour holiday will show him the real country. He will see the fields as a workshop instead of a playground. He will go back with a different feeling about our British heritage.' Would that it was feasible to do the same today, for a new generation of urban dwellers! Elsewhere in *Country Fair* that summer of 1951, Lady Patricia Ward explained how she rented a Suffolk farmhouse for £60 a year, and persuaded her trustees to release the money to equip and decorate it from top to bottom for £1,190. A village dweller, Evelyn Gibbs, described how mains water was at last being connected to her hamlet, provoking head-shaking among elderly inhabitants about the consequences of this reckless innovation, when main drains were still lacking.

Maurice Burton, the magazine's resident naturalist, lamented the decline of the dormouse, which he blamed upon the spread of grey squirrels. The famous amateur rider and breeder John Hislop wrote about the charms and horrors of owning a racehorse. Training fees were running at an extravagant seven guineas a week, plus 10 per cent of winnings. A jockey received five guineas for a losing ride and seven for a winner. It cost £100 to enter a horse for the Derby.

Here is some miscellaneous rural information from the same page: did you know that Northamptonshire is the only county of England to have nine others abutting on it? Or that until the late seventeenth century, July was called Jooly? Or that a Leicestershire acre used to be 2,308¾ square yards, and a Westmoreland one 6,760 square yards? In Anthony Armstrong's essay on Sussex, he quotes a disobliging comment on the county by one Dr Burton in 1751: 'Why is it that the oxen, the swine, women and all other animals are so long-legged in Sussex? May it be from the difficulty of pulling the feet out of so much mud?'

Thank God that these days we no longer have to make fuel briquettes out of coal dust and cement to heat the house, as some people did in 1951. I sympathise with the writer who lamented the miseries of driving a tractor in winter when cabs, heated or otherwise, were unheard of. Ploughing a furrow demanded a struggle with the elements almost as taxing as that involved in driving a horse team.

Constance Spry, who wrote a column on home entertaining, offered some tips for keeping food cool in a home without a frig (sic). She suggested hanging a damp cloth in the larder. Major Hugh Pollard contributed a recipe for cooking the harvest rabbit. Hugh, a notably eccentric friend of my father and author of that celebrated work *A History of Firearms*, was a keen cook in his leisure moments. In his youth after service in the First World War, he had seen action in Ireland as a Black and Tan.

More dubious still, he and one of his daughters assisted General Franco's secret passage from the Canaries to mainland Spain at the outset of that country's civil war. As a child, I was impressed by the manner in which the Pollard house near Petworth was strewn with exotic weapons, invariably loaded.

Today, I fear, an unamused constabulary would remove Hugh's Firearms Certificate in about five minutes, though most of the guns he kept about the house were not the kind for which one could have gained legal sanction even in those indulgent times. I was especially keen on his machine-pistols. Come to that, in *Country Fair* there is a set of photos of our family cottage, showing some of my father's guns standing unlocked in a rack at the foot of the stairs. My oh my, as Mole might have said, how the world has changed!

Yet some things are exactly the same. Roy Beddington, the angling writer and artist, painted a picture of chalk stream fishing in father's magazine which remains instantly recognisable to any of us: 'July is the month of the evening rise,' he observed. 'It is no time for the bungler or the over-excited, but a time for circumspection.' A host of new salmon flies has achieved primacy in our fishing lives since 1951, but the trout patterns which Beddington urged are the old faithfuls we still use today: Pale Wateries, Lunn's Particulars, Red and Sherry spinners, Blue-Winged Olives, Silver Sedges. 'It is time to make haste slowly,' he wrote, 'when every minute is precious, and every tangle and change of fly must be avoided.' These are sensations every fisherman still knows intimately, even if other experiences of that era — rationing and National Service, disastrous floods in East Anglia and black-market petrol – are mercifully unknown.

One of Reginald Arkell's verses decorated the pages of *Country Fair* that July of 1951:

> *The young men of the country*
> *They hurry up to town.*
> *In city ways they spend their days,*
> *A-running up and down.*
> *But the old men, the old men*
> *Can plough a furrow straight,*
> *In rain or shine, and still have time*
> *To lean upon a gate.*

Here, surely, is the greatest change since the days of father's old magazine: the pace of life has quickened. One of my family used to assert years ago that I would never be a proper countryman, because I did not make time to hang about and gossip with people across the counter of the village shop, or when passing them in the lanes. Those strictures were just. They apply to many others of a new generation who live in rural places. Even the ploughman whom Arkell celebrated above now has a computerised schedule to meet. We inhabit a far more comfortable rural world than our parents knew, in the days when even the grandest houses were underheated and hot water was a luxury. But our own era is a hastier one. Few people now dare admit to enjoying leisure to lean upon a gate. If they did so, an agent of the Health & Safety Executive would likely leap from behind a bush, pointing out the risk that it might fall on their toes and provoke litigation.

GELDART

2

Rhythm of the Seasons

*J*UST AS SWALLOWS wake up one morning and think: 'Gosh, I ought to be migrating,' so sportsmen sniff the late-summer air and reflect that it is time to get the gun out, maybe shoot a few clays, think about grouse if they are very lucky, or maybe the first partridges, wishing that they were wild greys. There is a rhythm about the sporting year, of which most of us become more conscious with each season of experience. This need not mean that one must be impatient for things to happen (though I have known fox-hunters who became catatonic between April and August). Rather, there is a sense of rightness about the moment when each phase of the cycle begins.

I do not think about fishing through the winter and early-spring months, nor even glance at my rods. In March and April, every spare moment is devoted to the garden. I do my best to get the borders into parade order before the river beckons, never entirely successfully. There is little temptation to fantasise about fishing when there is a nasty cold wind that must blow any fly, as well as any fisherman, off the water. Then comes a May morning when the breeze drops, spring sun warms the earth, and every instinct tells one to toss the net and bag into the back of the car, and nip down to the river. Its time has come, albeit usually a trifle late.

Much the same applies to salmon-fishing. A route to madness lies in brooding all summer about what may or may not be happening to familiar rivers when one is not oneself casting on them. I reach for my ear defenders when anyone rushes up at a party intending to describe record catches – or, for that matter, no catches at all – on the very beat one is due to visit a fortnight hence. Like-wise, I have abandoned an old habit of checking the weather on a given river day by day through the week before visiting it. What happens to Jack Smith on Thursday or Friday has absolutely no bearing upon what will happen to you or me the following Monday or Tuesday. As flies to wanton boys are we to the gods, and all that. Better just to turn up on the bank when the time comes, willing, eager and oblivious of recent history.

You will not be surprised to hear me confess, of course,

that it has taken fifty-nine years to become this phlegmatic creature. Patience is much easier when one enjoys many other things in life as well as sport. In my twenties I was obsessed to an unhealthy degree with shooting and fishing. These things meant more to me than anything else. I did not get many chances, and consoled myself by falling asleep every night reading about other people's sporting doings in country books and magazines. In the unlikely event that I had been given a choice between driven pheasant-shooting and a date with Diana Rigg, it would have been a tough call.

These days, like many sportsmen I find that the prospect which stirs most vivid excitement is the chance of a grouse. There is absolutely nothing which I would not cancel – weddings, funerals, christenings – to enjoy the privilege of missing those sublime birds. And even with grouse, I have trained myself not to think about them until a magical day in August, when one glances at the calendar and says, with studied carelessness: 'Oh well, better get ready. Yorkshire tomorrow.'

It is fortunate that grouse do not become operational until the garden is way over the top, the sweet peas hang limp and yellow, it is past time to spray the roses, and in the kitchen garden only runner beans will notice that one is away. My father believed that matters were divinely arranged so that grouse and partridges could be eaten with the last of those same beans, but this represented a touch of blasphemy on his part. What is true, I think, is that there comes a moment when we have had enough of the fag-end of summer, and embrace the coming of autumn: a new season, and in many respects the most

21

pleasing. Summers sometimes disappoint; autumns seldom do. The first ground frosts feel absolutely right as
one stands waiting for partridges – or, in a perfect world,
casting across Tweed in October or November. We might,
however, offer a petition to the Almighty to stop autumn
gales blowing leaves all over the river while one is trying
to cast a fly. It is enough to turn anyone into an atheist,
when the British seasons start overdoing things in the
fashion they have affected lately. Two years ago we could
not even fish Tweed in mid-October, because the river
was at a June drought level.

The pheasants that clatter aloft unscathed at the end
of an October partridge drive, taking flying lessons for
November, offer promise of good things to come. Yet
pheasant-shooting has suffered more than any other field
sport from upheavals in the climate. At midwinter we
want to shoot on cold, crisp days with a hard frost and
maybe even a little snow. That is what our forefathers
did. They wrote reams of doggerel extolling the beauties
of Christmas cock pheasants paddling about in the drifts.

Today, instead, we find ourselves turning out again and
again on mild, soggy days when nobody, including the
birds, really wants to do it. The abolition of our traditional
winter, especially in the south of England, is a blow to
field sports. There seems little chance that God will
change his mind and restore the old weather pattern –
indeed, if anything, matters will become more difficult as
the effects of global warming become ever more apparent.
The best we can hope for, these days, is a few sharp,
chilly days in January, towards the back end. I don't know
about you, but I have had enough by then. I feel ready

to stop, flee from England for a while, then turn to the garden again. I never sob for anything lost on the first of February. I am merely boundlessly grateful for the fun I have had, and happy to wait for it all to start again with the trout in late spring. 'To every thing there is a season,' wrote the sage in Ecclesiastes, 'and a time to every purpose under the heaven.' The old boy never said a truer word.

3

The River Keeper

$\mathscr{T}$HE GREAT Richard Walker once suggested dismissively that 'The most difficult thing about dry fly-fishing is to find somewhere to practise it.' He seems right up to a point. Now that so few of even the great south of England chalk streams offer truly wild fish, the art of the dry fly is diminished from the days Skues and Dunne knew. Yet for many of us, there remains a magic about fishing a river which is absent from still waters, save perhaps those of Scotland and Ireland. It seems worth every penny of the alarming cheques one must write, to savour the joy of casting beneath willows and among the rushes for a chalk stream trout. I would pay at least half the money each year merely for the privilege of walking the banks without a rod, watching the fish and the wildlife in summer. Even many professionals, I think, are drawn to a career in a fishery for the same reason.

The man who influences my own happiness on dry fly water more than any other lives in a modest cottage maybe half a mile from my own home, and a long cast from the river where he plies his trade – no, surely we should call it a profession. My daughter remarked the other day that she reckons only one in ten of the people she knows have jobs which they enjoy. This seems a fair guess. It does not represent mere sentiment to suggest that the career contentment quotient is higher in the country than in town. Those fortunate enough to forge a lifestyle working with nature are more likely to achieve happiness than people who merely massage money through their working days.

Our local river keeper, Stephen Jones on the Kennet at Chilton Foliat, seems one of the most fulfilled men I have ever met. Everybody who meets Stephen goes away muttering that he ought to be chairman of Microsoft or suchlike. He is forty-six, bright, decisive and fluent. But no, all his life he has wanted only to be a river keeper. This is fortunate for those of us who fish with him, because he is very good at it. And maybe it is also lucky for him. Here is a man who knows exactly what he wants, and knows that he has got it. He grew up in Southampton, where his father worked in a bank. It remains a mystery whence sprang his enthusiasm for running streams. The family used to visit the New Forest a lot, and as a teenager

Stephen did some pretty unsuccessful fishing on the public water of the Itchen estuary. But somehow the idea of working on a river got into his head, and stayed there. His father always said: 'Make sure you get a job you enjoy.'

A family farming friend mentioned that Sparsholt College was starting a fishery management course. Stephen enrolled for it. Meanwhile, at sixteen, when he left school – 'They didn't think I was the sharpest knife in the box' – he spent a year's apprenticeship on the Test at Broadlands. There, he says wryly, 'Working among men I did a lot of growing up very quickly.' After college he spent three years at Packington Fishery in Warwickshire, which he enjoyed but found very commercial: 'Rods really wanted their pound of flesh.' Then as now, he himself fished very little. Like gamekeepers who scarcely trouble to shoot, Stephen is a typical river keeper in that he gains his pleasure from living with the water, and from watching others cast. He is a good entomologist, but learned about insects from watching fly on the water, rather than from books. He knows his birds, is less confident with plants, 'But I'm still learning.'

He came to the Kennet in 1982, at a time when the Chilton Fishery was in poor health, after years in thrall to a Thames Conservancy policy designed to speed flow and improve field drainage for the only rural activity that seemed to matter in those days – growing corn. The estate syndicate could not sell all its rods, and was losing money. Stephen worked at increasing weed growth, putting bends back into the stream. He started rearing his own trout for stocking at the end of the season, 'Which is a big plus at the beginning of the next one, because you don't have a river full of gullible fish.'

Today, there is a long waiting list for rods, and Chilton is famously one of the prettiest stretches on the river. Stephen loves the variety of the fishing: 'Because the main river and the carriers are so different, there's always somewhere to get out of the wind, always somewhere to find a bit of shade, always somewhere you can get away on your own.' His own summer day starts at seven when he feeds the fish, walks the dogs and checks his fenn traps – he catches half a dozen mink a year. There are new rods to be shown around, and duffers like me who always need advice on flies. Towards evening there are also occasional poachers, 'white van men', usually in their early twenties, never alone, often plying a handline which they can drop in the water if they are spotted, to remove the evidence. They are the reasons for Tiger and Lizzie, Stephen's German shepherds, without which experience has warned him not to try consequences with intruders. He seldom bothers to call the police, because they come so slowly.

He says that his real pleasure in the job, beyond the beauty of the place, is meeting people. 'There used to be three old boys who came every Tuesday – a High Court judge, a former Hong Kong governor who'd been in Changi Jail, and a survivor of the sinking of the *Repulse*. I'd see them every lunchtime, and we'd sit down for a chat. They weren't boasting at all, but when you listened to those men and thought about what they'd seen and done . . .'

In summer, Stephen is a keen bowler for a local village cricket team. When there is no fishing in the winter, he loads and beats a bit. Out of season, he and his wife Fiona also travel, usually somewhere exotic. Two years ago it was Namibia, last time California. Fiona is Australian, from a country district a few hours outside Melbourne. They have been married for ten years, and she is a successful executive with Vodafone. Stephen is full of admiration for her swift rise: 'She's clever and she's Australian, which means she'll always say, "Let's give it a go!" We don't do that here, do we?'

I asked Stephen about the common mistakes he sees fishermen make. 'They don't *look* enough. They'll cast to a fish without noticing there's another one in between. Some people think that to be fishing, you've always got to be plying a rod. Time spent looking before you do anything is the trick. It's always a mistake to move too quickly, to rush around the river.' Does he never get restless? 'Never yet. I've not seen anywhere the grass is greener. Maybe towards the end of a season I might start to get a bit weary, then I see a rod coming down here for the first time, really excited about fishing. There are two Americans who cross the Atlantic every year, just to fish here. I think to myself: they're willing to come all that way, to be on this water. And I feel proud.'

His big beef, inevitably, is water abstraction. He fumes that the level of water which can be stolen upriver is assessed on the basis of the last calendar year, which means that 2003, for instance, was identified as wet because of what happened in January and February, despite the endless dry months that followed. In 2004, by early spring the river was at a June level, and matters have been worse in 2005. Yet Swindon was permitted to divert even more water than it was taking already – and none of this returned to the Kennet. Here is a sad and familiar story throughout the south of England, a grave threat to the future of our chalk streams. Whitehall planners continue to approve massive housing developments, heedless of how much water our modest river systems can spare for diversion to ever-growing conurbations. If the countryside of southern England loses its rivers – and several are desperately depleted – then a vital artery of rural life will be severed.

I suggested to Stephen that almost all the mistakes people make in life are things they miss out on, not things they do. He nodded. 'There was this chap who had a rod here – very successful businessman. In five years, he never got to the river once. He was just too busy. Now's he's dead. It seems such a waste, not to have done something you really like doing.' For himself, he says unhesitatingly that he has the life of his choice. He revels in feeling master of his own destiny: 'This is good. The world comes to you, rather than you having to go to it.' And those of us who fish with Stephen feel lucky that we should have the privilege of his company and his wisdom for many seasons yet.

4

Sunshine and Showers

Every real hunter, shooter and fisher accepts the weather as part of the game of chance that makes up sport. If we get soaked walking hedges in pursuit of a pheasant, the experience doubles the pleasure of lying in a bath afterwards with a whisky and a book. If our rivers and lakes were forever in perfect order, where would be the thrill and surprise about hooking a trout or salmon? G.E.M. Skues wrote a salutary short story about a man who died and found himself on a river where the fish were rising continuously. He thought he was in heaven, netting trout after perfect trout, until he grew to understand that this was an exquisite form of torture devised for the other place. Most of us practise field sports because we love to commune with wild things in wild places. The whimsy of the British weather is inseparable from the experience. Shooting high pheasants in a gale is difficult, because the target is usually travelling in two directions at once, but the thrill is doubled if you hit one of these superbirds.

The elements influence fishing even more decisively. William Blake observed wryly: 'The weather for catching fish is that weather, and no other, in which fish are caught.' One July Monday, I found myself plying a small double across a Scottish salmon river. The gillie frowned gloomily and observed: 'It's a fortnight since we had rain. We need the water up a couple of inches.' On Tuesday a fierce upstream wind made casting difficult even for experts. The gillie shook his head: 'The two best fishers I know go to sleep on the bank when there's an upstream wind.' On Wednesday, heavy thunderstorms stirred the current into cold chocolate soup: 'It should be great tomorrow if the rain stops and the river starts falling,' said the gillie in real excitement. The river rose a trifle on Thursday. On Friday, at last it was steady, though highly coloured. We caught some fish on big, bright flies, and thought eagerly of Saturday, when we would have the best beat on the river. But next morning there was more rain and more colour. We landed the odd salmon, but never reaped the sort of grand harvest that on Monday we had been sure must come.

Now, do not interpret this as a fisherman's whinge. We enjoyed a wonderful week on wonderful water and caught a respectable number of fish. I am simply making the point that ours was the sort of climatic experience every angler knows. Only once or twice in a lifetime do most of us get the chance to fish through several successive days of weather when fish and gauge marry, to yield a bonanza.

Shooting is a bit more reliable, but not much. About one day in three, conditions are the way we want them. The wind is blowing in the right direction, rain is holding off, the sun is not too bright. By contrast, there are those mornings in August when the sun is blazing magnificently, making it a pleasure to walk the hill, but young grouse receive no help from a breeze to lift them forward. After being flushed for the first time, they drop exhausted into the heather well in front of the butts, and refuse to get up again. September and October grouse are stronger and much more challenging, but by then the threat of mist or rain is never far distant. Few sporting experiences match the misery of receiving a priceless invitation to shoot grouse, then spending two days at the foot of the hill waiting for a 'clag' to lift.

Come pheasant-time, most of us reckon that a perfect December or January outing means an overcast day with some wind, when in Patrick Chalmers' phrase 'the snow-powdered stubble rings hard to the tread'. Yet a white landscape looks more romantic to guns than to keeper and beaters. It is a tough challenge, to persuade birds to leave patches of snow-covered brambles, to keep a beating line tramping a wood in which white lumps of wetness are flopping off the branches onto every beater's neck. On such days, the sight of dead pheasants precipitates in some of us a spasm of squeamishness. There is a pathos about a bird lying limp amid a cluster of feathers and pink spots of blood on the snow, which seldom troubles the senses in other conditions.

Yet in modern British winters, rather than snow we are likely to get mild, muddy, still, sunny days on which birds drift low over the guns with wings set, or others when torrential rain causes the water to run in streams down the barrel rib. Few of us can fib convincingly enough to make ourselves believe that we like competing in such conditions, when the stock of the gun is slipping in the hand and we are struggling to see coveys or flushes through the squalls. Gene Kelly may have enjoyed singing in the rain, but how many of us, deep down, like shooting in it? On a Saturday morning not long back, the phone rang in Hastings Towers at 8 a.m. Glancing out of the window at a torrential downpour, with more of the same promised all day, I experienced a surge of hope that my pheasant host was ringing to cancel. Not a chance, of course. Already some guns had been in their cars for half an hour, while beaters and pickers-up were congregating from all over the region. Shooting dates are fixed six or nine months before they take place. Not even a death in the family is likely to change them.

About here, hardy veterans of the Norfolk coast, the Northumbrian hills, the Cornish valleys, start muttering to each other: 'Not much of a sportsman this chap Hastings, is he? Doesn't like getting his feet wet!' Yet my purpose in these jottings is sometimes to suggest sentiments which lots of people secretly share, but don't like to admit. Of course we are all out there doing our thing, even when cats and dogs are plummeting down. But most of us, in such circumstances, wish we were at home in front of the fire. The only case for shooting in the rain is that, like looking at other people's holiday snaps, it is so wonderful when it is over.

Modern clothing is much more effective than the kit of fifty years ago. Encased in thermals and Gore-Tex, it should be possible to avoid ever being cold or wet again. That is, if one stays perfectly still. The problem about shooting is that it requires moving our arms and legs, sometimes quite energetically. Every extra sweater makes it marginally harder to swing a gun. On a really rough day, those of us who affect enough clothing to impress a moon-walker find it difficult to raise a flask to our lips, never mind take aim at a rocketing pheasant. A majority of shooters perform best when wearing least – no, I don't mean quite that, but shirtsleeves anyway. We become slower and clumsier with each layer of protection.

Unless it is very cold, I never wear gloves in the rain, because they become such wretched things when water-logged. That leaves one stumping between drives clutching a dog skewer caked in mud, cartridge bag and shooting stick ditto, wiping a hand disconsolately on the grass before putting sticky fingers on the gun. My smart friends have nowadays abandoned spectacles in favour of contact lenses, especially for sport. They say that these make all the difference in the world when the heavens open, or one is trying to woo another wife. Yet goggles have been part of me for so long now that I can't face changing.

Fine, misty rain is worst for sporting spectacle-wearers.

For the first half-hour, one dries one's glasses occasionally on a handkerchief. Thereafter, the hanky becomes so sodden that it is past doing the business. I simply peer out upon a universe shrouded in wet. When a blurred flying object appears, I point the gun roughly in its direction and fire, confident that even if it is an owl or a sparrow-hawk, there is not the smallest chance it will suffer any damage. I often wonder how wildfowlers manage to kill anything, when they do not bother to venture out of doors unless there is a Force Eight gale and raindrops are battering their camouflage suits with the impact of tin tacks. I have always admired wildfowlers, while being a little frightened of them, in the way that soldiers fear officers who want to win the VC. I cherish an uneasy apprehension that a friendly wildfowler will one day cajole me into sharing his experiences. I prefer to read books about them, to savour the full pleasure of not being on the saltings myself. In 1916, the Germans placed an advertisement in the US press, designed to deter inter-ventionists: 'Americans! If you are thinking of participating in the European war and wish to sample the sensations of combat, you may do so without leaving home. Dig a six-foot hole in your garden. Half-fill it with water. Then live in it for a few weeks in mid-winter on a diet of cold food and muddy coffee, paying a lunatic to fire machine-guns at you.' If one leaves out the machine-guns, that seems a pretty vivid description of wildfowling.

I have never asked a pheasant how it feels about being asked to put on a sporting performance in a deluge, but its demeanour usually leaves one in little doubt. Pheasants that have been soaked overnight scamper about in front of the beaters, looking as if they had just emerged from a swimming pool. If eventually shooed into flight, the sensible ones beat their wings half-heartedly a few times, then settle back where they came from, pleading exemption under Conditions of Labour legislation. True, I attended a heavy-rain high-bird shoot in Wiltshire last season where the pheasants performed more convincingly than the guns, but since the poor brutes were being driven off precipices, they were not given much choice. One needs only to look at a wet dead pheasant on the game cart to know that it was not feeling its best even before encountering a pattern of no. 6 shot. The truth is that we should not shoot in heavy rain, because it is not fair on the birds. It is a bit like asking a horse to race with a couple of stone overweight, or a sprinter to perform in ski boots. Some of you will think that I am being a bit – well, wet about all this. Maybe so, but the truth is that when we launch a day's shooting in heavy rain, we are suiting our own administrative convenience or financial imperative, rather than measuring the quality of sport.

Yet after a morning of downpours on a grouse moor, all debts of discomfort are repaid if the showers clear by afternoon, the sun bursts through, the dogs shake themselves dry, the heather steams. Even the midge hatch seems bearable if God lets up on us before the last drive. Perversely, it is often the days when one has battled with the elements, casting into a cutting wind or striving to push the barrels after birds streaking across the line, that stick fondly in the memory. Sport is least interesting when it is easy. The quarry we pursue must live through all the days and seasons. We do not seek to share the full rigour of its experience, but we can at least go to meet it halfway. Even when I am moaning, I try to remind myself that a fair-weather sportsman is no sportsman at all.

5

The Young Entry

I HAVE BEEN a young gun now for, oh, forty-something years. I have started to think of myself as quite an experienced young gun. I seem to get more shooting days than I managed a few seasons ago, in the sixties. What was that you said? Surely not. A Scottish pub landlord asked only the other evening, 'What can I get for you, young man?' I felt quite bucked. It is unkind to suggest that he was being satirical. One day last summer, however, I found myself in a line with half a dozen shots who were indisputably younger young guns than me. They were accompanied by wives who clapped their hands prettily as they fired, and babies in pushchairs. One of the team said: 'I couldn't get to sleep last night, I was so excited about shooting grouse today.' His words pricked my heart, touching memories two or three decades old. I remembered exactly that sense of excitement and appre-hension. Ruefully, I recognised that even if I am not yet an old gun, in the eyes of that man's generation I am a Boer War veteran – well, at least a Falklands one, which is almost the same thing.

My father imbued me with a passionate enthusiasm for shooting and fishing, without providing many opportuni-ties, because he lacked the means. In my teens I walked-up pheasants or grouse maybe half a dozen times a year, and shot pigeon a few more. At the age of twenty-four I took half a gun in a pheasant shoot, and began to rent a dogging grouse moor in Sutherland. Nowadays, if my children started doing those things on incomes as slender as mine was, I would have them put under medical supervision. Friends and even relations assumed that if I owned a sports car and took a Scottish shooting lodge, I must be richer than they thought. In truth, sporting *folies de gran-deur* brought me within a whisker of bankruptcy. Yet I can never forget the euphoria of those wonderful early sporting days, when every grouse that rose from the heather seemed a miracle of beauty, and each shot at a driven pheasant was an adventure. Young sportsmen, like young everything elses, experience the summits of joy and the depths of despair, an emotional topography which the river of time flattens by middle age.

It is a relief to have left behind the financial horrors of those early years, which dominated my overdraft. When we quit Sutherland to drive south after summer idylls in the seventies, around Dingwall I began to think about the bank manager. By the time we passed Carlisle, I was wondering what I could sell to pay the bills. You may say that a real sportsman doesn't think too much about what things cost. I don't agree. Many of us, especially the young, become upset if we have a seriously bad draw on a paying day we know we cannot really afford. And in those early years I became almost hysterical about wasted opportunities when I shot really badly, as I usually did.

One of the greatest pleasures of middle-aged shooting is that one is more relaxed. If the weather is bloody on Monday, one knows that there will probably be sunshine on Saturday. Belatedly, I am even learning not to mind too much if the birds flock to the next peg, and I miss the ones over my own head. Does this represent maturity, or a loss of that 'edge' one needs to shoot well? You tell me.

An aspect of getting older is that my fear of doing something dangerous has increased, rather than diminished. Many of us, once in a season or two, take a shot that brings on a sudden cold chill as the report dies away. Perhaps it is because one has fired low at a partridge with a hedge behind it, perhaps when one suddenly feels uncertain where the nearest stop is. One afternoon last season, I was bawled out by a head keeper's wife for taking an overhead grouse after the first horn had gone. I thought the shot was perfectly safe. She did not. In these matters the home team is always right. I apologised, and meant it. Whereas our great-grandparents made jokes about peppering beaters or shooting a loader, nowadays we all know that no accident with a gun is remotely funny. The deep public suspicion of firearms and field sports, which is a fact of modern life, makes us morbidly sensitive about doing anything that might increase it.

In my twenties I filled our home with sporting prints and later watercolours and paintings, as had my father. I recently heard Malcolm Innes, a veteran of the trade, say that sales of sporting art – at the popular end of the market anyway – are languishing. Malcolm suggests that this is because the young are simply not buying pictures of the kind we all loved: Thorburn and J.C. Harrison prints, Balfour-Browne stalking sketches. He suspects – and my instinct is that he is right – that while the new generation likes field sports well enough, few twenty-somethings embrace them as consuming passions. Perhaps this is partly because shooting is now almost prohibitively expensive and hard to come by for their generation. When I was twenty-two, the owners of a girls' school near our home in Hampshire let me roam its woods, potting the odd pheasant. I can't imagine anyone these days giving a young man with a gun that sort of licence. In the south of England rough shooting has become almost unobtainable. Yet we should recognise that driven shooting is a bastard extravagance for relatively rich men. Walking-up game with dog and gun is, and always should be, the core of sport.

But then I think again of that eager thirty-something-year-old I met last summer, who couldn't sleep for his excitement at the prospect of the morrow on the moor. The passion persists among some of the young. Our job – the responsibility of the not-so-young – is to see that the next generation is given the opportunities to keep alive the sporting heritage. George Eliot wrote: 'If youth is the season of hope, it is often so only in the sense that our elders are hopeful about us.' Yet the young must be given the chance to experience the magic and catch the bug, to become steeped in the enthusiasm we have known.

Children's shoots may sometimes be alarming experiences, but they are bedrock for the future. In our family we continue to give an annual outing that name, though all those involved are now in their twenties. My son and daughter ask three or four friends apiece to a day which I take for them on a nearby estate. Roughly the same team has turned up every year for the past six or seven. Port – which none of my own age-group seems to drink at all – is consumed in prodigious quantities at dinner the night before the action. Indeed, the general alcohol intake would have commanded respect at a Roman bacchanalia, though I don't mind when the young are not driving anywhere. Some subsequently sleep in beds, others doss wherever they can find a corner of the house – we never ask.

Marshalling the guns next morning, one might suppose that they had regressed to a common age of about six. Waking and feeding them, ensuring that they are properly equipped, demands a large nursery staff, rather than just me and a frying pan. Each must be quizzed before setting out, to ensure that he or she has Wellingtons, gloves, jackets, firearms. I warned two of the party to make sure they put plenty of 20-bore cartridges in the cars. We arrived at the shooting lodge to find that they had brought only a case of 12s. How do they get to the cinema on the right day, never mind earn livings?

I carry a radio rather than a gun at these affairs, taking my orders from the keeper, who fortunately knows us well and possesses a keen sense of humour. I lay on the safety warnings with special energy. A few years ago, one twenty-year-old gun – from a shooting family – terrified me. I saw him twice try to shoot a pheasant almost head-high in front before I reached his peg and lacerated him. He was not on the list this year, thank goodness. The first two drives were memorable for producing the worst exhibition of shooting I can remember since the guns were about twelve. On a sharp, cold day with a touch of wind, the partridges flew like smoke. A barrage of fire poured skywards. My dog sprang expectantly at each detonation, hoping for something to retrieve. Not a chance, ducky.

I stood behind my daughter. At the age of twenty-eight, she still cherishes a delusion that she can pick up a gun once a year, having spurned all offers of an outing at the shooting school, and expect birds to fall down. 'You're six feet behind every bloody one!' I exclaimed, relishing the knowledge that nobody present had seen me shoot lately. 'Chill out, Daddy,' said the daughter scathingly. She was raising the gun so hesitantly that the bird was twenty yards behind the peg before she pressed a trigger. Then she stood contemplating its undamaged passage into the distance, expecting it to expire as an act of will, instead of reloading for the next flush. The boys, if one can still call them that, were throwing prodigious quantities of lead into the sky for not much better results.

After the second drive, the keeper announced with relish over the radio that 330 shots had been fired. Thirty-seven birds had been picked up. I pressed the handset and demanded, in front of the team, whether he had seen a worse showing this season. 'No,' he said decisively, amid a howl of mirth from the guns. In fairness, most of the boys get no more shooting than I did at their age, which was not a lot. But some do have practice. One of their daddies, indeed, features on best-shots-in-Britain lists. I said that they seemed to be hitting less than last year. 'It was the port,' they replied, attacking mid-morning sloe gin, soup and sausages as if they had not seen a square meal in a month.

The great thing about being boss of a day like this is that one can profess omniscience, in the absence of sceptics who know my own form. 'By now,' I told them confidently after the third drive, 'a team of Chelsea Pensioners armed with walking sticks could have two hundred in the bag.' One of our beaters had a seizure at the spectacle of a female gun, an old friend of my daughter and not a bad shot, trying to finish off a wounded pheasant by clubbing it to death with her gun butt. She suffered girlish scruples not about shooting it, but about wringing its neck or even whacking it against a tree. I told her that she should adopt my father's favoured method, crushing its skull in her teeth. She looked like one of those young ladies in Victorian novels who came over all funny when somebody mentioned the word manure.

For us control freaks, the hardest part of entertaining the young alongside one's own offspring is to keep one's mouth shut. The spectacle of my son pouring himself a lunchtime gin of a size that would have impressed our dear late Queen Mother caused me to retire into a corner and gnash my teeth before rejoining the throng. I have given up knowing what does, or does not, constitute reasonable behaviour in the next generation. And in my heart, I was pleased with the son for shooting quite decently. A couple of days earlier, standing on the next peg at another shoot, he had wiped my eye at quite a tall pheasant. Most fathers like to see this happen, and I am no exception.

At the drive after lunch, the team pulled itself together and shot a bit better, though the keeper murmured to me that the birds were so wet he thought the dogs had caught several. The 'children' had adored every second of it. They departed leaving behind the usual random assortment of property. One year, a boy left a gun case – quite a good one. Despite ringing round the usual suspects, no one claimed it, so it has joined the Hastings equipment collection. I would murder any child of mine who left a gun case on the other side of England, but maybe some families have so much sporting kit that they don't miss trifles.

Every year I ask myself whether I can afford to go on entertaining the children's friends in this way. Nobody did it for me. But nowadays we all know that if we don't help them to get started, there is no way they can make it on their own. I guess I shall go on forking out as long as the bank manager allows. I see our children's shoot as a minuscule contribution to ensuring that the marvellous ritual of field sports survives through the next generation, and the new century.

6

Life at the Trough

FOR ALL MY part-rural upbringing, it took me much too long to appreciate that the best things to eat are to be found in the countryside. Until at least twenty, I cherished a delusion that meals came from shops. In those long-gone, pre-Fayed days, Harrods was a focus of middle-class London life. From the age of about eighteen months onwards, we met in its banking hall, had our hair cut by its barbers, bought our treats from the toy department, stationery from the stationery department and food, not unexpectedly, from the food department. The Hastingses were anything but rich but, since my mother spent her days editing magazines and organising fashion shoots, food was ordered by telephone and delivered weekly by green van, each item exquisitely wrapped in grey paper and tied with string.

I was born just after the Second World War. Food rationing, together with spasmodic black-marketeering for tea, meat and suchlike, persisted until I was seven. A lifelong enthusiasm for cheap sweets stems, I fancy, from the fact that when I was in rompers our allowance was only about four ounces of bull's-eyes and gobstoppers a week. Nonetheless, at home we ate pretty well, managing about four heavy meals a day. Nursery delicacies, administered by my adored old Yorkshire nanny in her starched grey overalls, included bread and sugar, bread with hundreds and thousands, lots of steamed puddings and Bird's custard. Oh yes, and there was Shippam's potted meat paste, a great treat. Part of the fun was to make toast on a fork in front of the nursery electric fire, a process which caused me to fuse the element with irksome frequency. With hindsight, it is puzzling that I was not electrocuted.

There was a famous chain of teashops named Fuller's, which produced its own branded cakes. Heaven for every boarding schoolboy of the 1950s was to receive one in a parcel. Fuller's walnut was the most famous, but personally I preferred Fuller's chocolate cake. My mother occasionally reminded me that they cost six shillings apiece and therefore counted as luxury food, but in my prep school prime I could demolish a two-pound Fuller's cake single-handed, at one sitting. We occasionally drank Coca-Cola, but irrationally Kia-Ora orange squash and Lucozade were considered healthier for us. At about twelve I acquired a secret passion for that heavily marketed second-hand car salesman's drink Babycham. It was very sweet, mildly alcoholic, and could be bought illicitly at the back door of the village pub for one shilling and three pence for a small bottle.

We ate a lot of fish, which came from the wonderful Knightsbridge fish shop opposite Harrods where the spoils of the sea lay on an open marble slab, presided over by a genial giant with a red nose, blue-and-white-striped apron and straw hat. The butcher, too, wore a straw hat as his badge of office. I was reared in the belief that all right-thinking Englishmen lived off huge chunks of bleeding meat, a vision that has never faded. In those days meat seemed, and indeed was, very expensive. Fillet and sirloin seldom entered our house. The Sunday joint was usually a second-division cut like topside. At grown-up dinner parties my mother favoured crown of lamb, the cutlets primly decorated with little paper coronets. These were followed by the Hastings household's absolutely favourite pudding – chocolate profiteroles with whipped cream, created with sublime artistry by my mother's German cook, Martha. The family always managed to be broke, in a very English middle-class way. That is to say, we lived amid chronic gloom about money, but everybody seemed to chuck it about.

When I was shipped off to prep school at the age of eight, my father inaugurated a custom designed to soften the blow. On the first day of every term, before delivering me to the 3 p.m. train from Paddington, he took me to a West End restaurant for lunch. His opening shot was Le Caprice, then as now in Arlington Street. He introduced me to Mario, the head waiter, asserting reverently that I would find him one of the most important people in my life. Father also pointed out stars such as Noël Coward and David Niven. With some help from Mario, whom even as a stripling I found pretty oleaginous, the French menu was interpreted

None of this diminished in the smallest degree my misery and terror about being removed from Rutland Gate SW7 to a punishment camp in Berkshire named Horris Hill. There, prowess on the playing field was the only virtue deemed worthy of applause, and certain masters did not trouble to conceal their enthusiasm for the prettier small boys. At the Caprice, when I asked tremulously for an ice cream and was presented instead with a sorbet, I perceived deliberate deceit and collapsed into hysterical sobs. If father had thought to sweeten the bitter pill of Horris Hill with a mere restaurant luncheon, he failed. I was still seething when I boarded the Hogwarts Express.

Yet restaurant lunches persisted on those black days at the beginning of each term. Once we went to Simpson's-in-the-Strand, where we ate beef off the trolley and my father instructed me on the importance of tipping the carver half a crown. We tried the Ivy, where I was briefed about all manner of writers and literary agents to be seen at the tables, none of whose names meant a thing to me. I much preferred Lyons Corner House in Coventry Street, the huge multiple restaurant complex where we usually patronised the Seven Stars, which served delicious roasts with jacket potatoes for around fifteen shillings (75p) a head. When I first started taking girls out, the Seven Stars got a lot of my custom. I never bothered to ask my dates how they felt about roasts. I just assumed, like many of my generation, that you could never go wrong with meat. The most satisfactory meal I can recall as a teenager comprised a prawn cocktail and a fillet steak, with a second prawn cocktail to follow. 'I knew you were eccentric when you came in,' said the waitress gloomily.

In those days I spent about 150 per cent of my weekly income on entertaining girls. At eighteen, I remember giving one of them a notably lavish, overpriced dinner at a restaurant in Swallow Street near Piccadilly Circus named the Pipistrello. She didn't display the smallest sexual gratitude at the time, but I suppose the evening wasn't an entirely futile extravagance, since she is now my wife.

The restaurants which won my heart – and for many adult years my custom – were those great fisheries: Wheeler's in Old Compton Street, the Carafe behind Harrods and the Vendôme in Dover Street. They were owned by an exuberant friend of my father's named Bernard Walsh, for whom oyster was a middle name. Bernard staged annual seaside parties at Colchester to celebrate the opening of the season, from which his guests returned sick but happy. Father belonged to a notorious lunching group named the Thursday Club, which met every week on the top floor of Wheeler's, and was regularly denounced by gossip columnists as a den of all manner of misbehaviour. Its star members in the early 1950s were Prince Philip, Baron the 'society photographer', actors Peter Ustinov and James Robertson Justice, the Marquess of Milford Haven, mouth organist Larry

Adler and *Daily Express* editor Arthur Christiansen. That they all got very drunk was not in doubt. I am sceptical about whether much else went on. I was put down for the Thursday Club at birth, but sadly it collapsed before I was old enough to participate.

Any day of the week, Wheeler's was my father's home from home, and it became mine. The menu boasted twenty variations on Dover sole. My own favourite was Normande, served with a wine and grape sauce. Lunch for two cost about £3 including wine in the early 1960s, and was eaten huddled at tiny tables which became a trifle cramped when two members of the Hastings family were in possession. It was all so wonderfully English. There was no nonsense about *nouvelle cuisine* at Wheeler's. Indeed, I am doubtful whether in its heyday any mere foreigner would have got a table.

About now, thoughtful readers may ask: if the Hastings family was skint, how did they manage to do such grand eating? The same way they do now, silly. Expenses. Since both my parents were employed by media organisations, I doubt if they ever paid for a restaurant meal out of their own pockets. We had nothing in banks save overdrafts, but the Lord (Beaverbrook or Rothermere) was always good for a glass of champagne and a lobster. My father's epicurean masterclasses triumphantly succeeded in one respect. They induced in me an enthusiasm for expensive food which has never faded. Likewise, when I started working and living in a flat on my own, I simply summoned rations by telephone from Harrods. I had no idea how else food might be obtained. The consequence, as you might surmise, was an impressive series of financial

51

smashes in my early twenties. One of them was retrieved only by a handsome legacy from dear old nanny, when she passed on to the great nursery in the sky after seventeen years' hard labour with the Hastingses.

I once observed at a dinner party in the 1990s that I wished I had discovered back in 1964 or thereabouts that a girl was just as likely to go to bed with you if you bought her a hot dog as if you took her to Wheeler's. This caused a middle-aged woman to shout from the far end of the table: 'Rubbish! If a bloke gave me a good dinner, I used to feel I owed him one.' I said how much I wished that we had met thirty years earlier.

Nowadays, my culinary life has changed out of recognition. In deepest west Berkshire, our family try to be living exemplars of The Good Life. Scarcely a restaurant features in the programme any more. At Hastings Towers we live off the land, though this is by no means a universally popular policy. About once a week, my wife stands by the back gate crying out towards open country: 'Mr Fox! Mr Fox! Where are you? Come on in!' This is a demo directed at me. It is designed to emphasise how tiresome Penny finds our chickens, and especially the bother of feeding and watering them. 'When did you last hear of Marks & Spencer running out of eggs?' she demands crossly. I find it soothing to see a few hens scratching about in a pen. They may not be very bright, nor very rewarding conversationalists, but if you put layer's mash in at one end, something useful emerges at the other.

In our rustic domain, the chicken controversy is only one manifestation of a wider debate: how much husbandry can we take? If we profess to be country-dwellers and sportsmen, how far does it behove us to live off the landscape, to bottle and dry and freeze the spoils of chase and garden as our ancestors did? We eat a lot of game. I would be happy to exist on a permanent diet of semi-raw grouse, if others about the house shared my enthusiasm, which they do not. Many women find grouse too gamey. There is also domestic resistance to my views about how long birds should be hung, and to my theory that a few maggots contribute added protein, a view rigorously contested by the European Union in its latest regulations on the marketing of game meat.

I release a lot of the trout I hook, sometimes deliberately, simply because nobody in the house will eat it more than three or four times in a summer. It is a problem with fish that until one tastes them it is impossible to guess how they will turn out. Some are delicious pink things, rich with shrimp, while others prove to have grey flesh, and to taste only of pellets. The latter is bad enough if one is eating alone, sorely embarrassing if there is company. Even salmon cannot be relied upon, unless they are fresh-run. In ignorant youth I killed a lot of stale fish for smoking or fishcakes, before realising that a horrible old red thing will always taste that way, however one processes it. We try to eat every fish within a month or two of committing it to the freezer, before it dries out.

We are fanatical consumers of garden produce, our big extravagance. Even the crudest calculation by most honest amateur gardeners reveals that one could have fruit and vegetables delivered weekly from Fortnum & Mason more cheaply than growing one's own. I speak as one who has just put in a new fruit cage. Only around 2035 might the strawberries and raspberries grown therein pay back the price of the frame. But that is not the point, as we peasants tell each other. The issues are quality and self-sufficiency.

The quality bit starts looking shaky when we contemplate our asparagus. It is thin stuff compared with the fat, rich stalks from the pick-your-own place down the road. We struggle on, however, pouring onto the soil ever more dung at £65 a load, together with chemical fertilisers in industrial quantities. Cabbages, beetroot, onions, leeks and the rest flourish mightily on our acres and are eaten in bulk. The gardener cheats, however, by leaving every week at the back door baskets groaning with produce from his own allotment, rather in the spirit that Nigella Lawson might display a cake before the camera, saying smugly: 'And here's one I prepared earlier.' He is especially eager to produce earlier samples of species which I have planted with my own hands. This twists the knife, or rather the trowel, about my horticultural limitations. In a cynical moment, my wife suggested that we could simply get the gardener to maintain regular deliveries from his own patch, saving the expense of doing our own tillage as well. Shame on her.

My favourite technical innovation, purchased four years ago, is an apple press. Every season now, we squeeze and freeze about forty litres of apple juice, lovingly stored in plastic milk containers. As I point out, this also saves the gardener from having to clear up thousands of windfalls. As Penny points out, however, using an apple press requires physical effort matching that of child labour in a coal mine circa 1840. I am bathed in sweat after an hour of turning the great screw, manhandling the truckloads of fruit needed to produce a litre or two of juice. I find the process therapeutic, pleasingly Hardyesque. Others, however, gaze wistfully down the road that leads to the supermarket as they mop their brows in the autumn sunshine.

We are self-sufficient in firewood, thanks partly to fallen branches, and partly to the fact that we don't use a lot when we cuddle the Aga all winter. Like most men, I thoroughly enjoy an outing with a chainsaw and a chunk of fallen timber, though at least once a season I give myself a fright, using the saw up a tree. There was a delicate moment when I severed a big ash limb. As it plunged to the ground, the lightened butt sprang upwards, trapping my arm between itself and a rung of the ladder on which I stood, twenty feet above the ground. It took a lonely ten minutes to disengage myself, during which I contemplated my immortal soul, and reflected that these experiences are not quite so bracing at fifty-something as they seemed at twenty-something. I got no sympathy indoors, either.

Most of us get lazier with the passage of years. I no longer make my own sloe gin, nor point chimneys, hang wallpaper or demolish pigeons in the garden with a .22. The more expensive tools I install in the workshop, the less likely I am to use them for ambitious woodworking of the kind I enjoyed thirty years ago. Yet it still gives pleasure to see things around house and garden which one has built or repaired with one's own hands. The consequence of a childhood during the rationing era is that I never feel entirely comfortable about the state of the household, unless it is provisioned for a siege. In my complacent bed at night, I go to sleep counting not sheep but game in the three freezers, poised in the epicurean waiting room en route to my plate. I do not despair of learning to pot my own shrimps. We would have to call our Hastings Towers version The Quite Good Life rather than the whole package, but we do our rustic best.

7

Duffers' Days

$\mathcal{N}$OT LONG AGO, I watched a young girl cast a fly on a Scottish salmon river. Her line fell in a bundle amid the stream, and straightened only five, ten seconds after landing – which of course meant that it was unlikely to impress a fish for half the time it was crossing potentially active water. My heart bled for her. Yet I need not have worried. She caught a fish. This turned my mind to a general question. We know that a good dry fly trout fisherman will always catch more than a bad one. Unless one is plying a river in the mayfly season, or addressing oneself to tame fish lately released, the fine caster prevails over the coarse one, because presentation is all.

Yet different rules apply to salmon fishing. Again and again, we see novices and indifferent fishers achieving startling success. I have been a beneficiary myself. Many years ago in Sutherland, I remember looks of pained disgust on the faces of others in the party, who were enamoured neither of my company nor of my casting, as they saw me land an indecent number of salmon. For sentimental reasons I was fishing with a huge old green-

57

heart Hardy of my father's. Returning with a fish one night, I heard a fellow-guest mutter disgustedly: 'And with that rod, too.' In short, I was lucky.

Luck can carry an incompetent fisher a long way on a smallish salmon river, with good water. A long cast is seldom necessary. Most beats contain pools dominated by rushes of fast water, which will rectify a poor cast very quickly, whipping the fly round into touch. Maunsell, author of one of my favourite sporting books, *The Fisherman's Vade Mecum*, urges that one should never retrieve a bad cast, but leave it to complete its course. That cast can never be exactly repeated, he observes. Every now and again, however unjustly, a tangle of line will catch a fish, because some whim of the water will advance the fly in a tempting fashion. I follow Maunsell's advice religiously, and never try to recover a poor line.

On a big river a better caster will usually catch more salmon, because he or she will cover more taking places. On the Tay not long ago, in a nasty wind, telepathically I knew exactly what my boatman was thinking: 'Unless that big bugger can throw a better line than this, he won't catch many fish here.' He was right. I landed a grilse which took in streamy water directly behind the boat, but my attempts to cover a distance remained unconvincing. The salmon thought so, too. One is sometimes rescued by a wind, which can flatter casting outrageously. But it is a wry law of fishing that most winds blow the wrong way. It is dispiriting to see flies whipped round behind the line, and not infrequently knotted as well. Those are the moments when I hate suffering under a gillie's eye. Alone, I can sometimes sort myself out, and make the best of a bad blow. With sceptical eyes present, however, I can never do so. Worst of all in these circumstances, the gillie finds an excuse to take the rod himself for a moment, and flicks the fly effortlessly across the flood as if that accursed zephyr did not exist. Those are the times when I am tempted to take up bowls.

At low water, the quality salmon fisherman comes into his own. The duffer is confounded. When the flow dwindles, the river shrinks to expose acres of rocks and pebbles on the bed, the man and woman who know what they are doing can achieve amazing results, while the rest of us are put in our places. It is an object lesson to watch a really gifted caster place a fly, and move a fish, when we lesser mortals despair of stirring the surface, save to drive salmon into flight. I fished the Naver for many years, sometimes in conditions verging on hopeless. A party fishing the next beat from us never seemed to lack something on the account. 'The Farquharsons are the best fishers on the river,' our gillie observed approvingly, refraining from comment upon our own doings. Likewise, I met an exceptionally skilful friend fishing a neighbouring beat of the Naver during a boiling, arid July when our own party had despaired. I found that he had taken two salmon out of a mere puddle of a pool at 6 o'clock that morning. I too was fishing at 6 a.m., but without success.

I recently suggested to Angus, a notably skilful gillie, that in all conditions and all rivers, over a period a good fisher might take 35 per cent more fish than a bad one, casting for the same number of hours. Angus thought that was about right. Contrast this with trout fishing, where a really poor caster is likely to catch nothing at all except maybe in poor light on an evening rise. That guesstimate about salmon fishing also takes account of the vagaries of playing fish which one has been fortunate enough to hook. Of course, someone who instinctively does the right things is more likely to land his catch than one who lets the line go slack, drops his rod point or whatever. But even the finest fishermen lose their share of fish, especially grilse, when these are taking short.

There seems no correlation between the quality of the man or woman behind the rod and the manner in which fish get hooked, and stay that way – with smaller fish anyway. As many gillies will assert that a salmon has got off because it was played too soft, as played too hard. Unless the fisher makes a fundamental error, once again luck seems the principal influence upon the outcome of the contest, though unsurprisingly the bigger the fish, the more likely is a bungler to mess up the landing of it.

A further interesting twist to the argument concerns the matter of morning or afternoon fishing. A gillie whom I respect said the other day: 'Three-quarters of fish are taken in the morning. If the truth be known, you're wasting your time casting a fly between one and six.' Angus said that he himself, when he fishes, only goes out between 6 and 9 a.m. As he catches seventy salmon a year to his rod, which is a lot in Britain these days, I found myself brooding a good deal about what he said.

My gamebook represents the most efficient aspect of my sporting activities, sustained with morbid precision since I was nine. I have been looking back through it, to see how far Angus's opinion seems justified by my own experience. Here are rough tallies of some British salmon-fishing expeditions over the past fifteen years, from which blanks for obvious reasons are excluded: Tweed five fish a.m., five p.m.; Helmsdale six fish a.m.; Helmsdale three a.m., one p.m.; Helmsdale two a.m., three p.m.; Tweed four a.m., two p.m.; Naver five a.m., two p.m.; Naver seven a.m., four p.m.; Laxford six a.m., two p.m.; Naver six a.m., one p.m.; Laxford three a.m., three p.m.; Naver seven a.m., four p.m.

Examining the afternoon totals more carefully, two-thirds of those salmon were caught after 6 p.m., more often than not because earlier conditions were too bright for convincing fishing. Angus's views about the merits of taking a doze on the bank after lunch start to sound plausible. It seemed to matter much less on Tweed than on the northern rivers whether one was fishing morning or afternoon. I guess – and as usual with all matters pertaining to salmon fishing, here I am simply tossing out a few ideas to have them shot down by readers from their own experience – this reflects the fact that I fish Tweed during the short late autumn days, while I have usually visited Sutherland rivers in July or August.

I like fishing alone, early on summer mornings, if I know a river well enough to find my way about. There is a special thrill about hooking and landing a salmon without assistance, in playing out a little sporting drama amid the lonely majesty of the surrounding hills. I know some houses which discourage guests from this practice on the grounds that it is anti-social, and upsets gillies who start at 9 a.m. My attitude, however, is that we are there to catch fish if we can. Left to my own devices, all meals including breakfast would be eaten on the river between casts.

Some people also offer practical objections to early fishing – that one loses two or three hours' sleep to no great purpose, because the salmon seldom wake up much before 9 a.m. I come home from four out of five early-morning raids empty-handed, but the fifth success pays for all. On hot days, there is surely no better prospect of catching a fish than in the hours before the sun climbs high. In October and November, with relatively little time in which to fish, it is not difficult to keep casting from nine to five. My own slender afternoon scores in the summer partly reflect the fact that, more often than not, I fall asleep after lunch. Even when I am casting a fly in the torrid p.m.s, if there is little action, concentration flags. It is in the mornings that one goes at it like a tiger, fishing with deadly intent as long as there is water under the fly. Most fishermen possess an ability to convince themselves that a morning pool is virgin, that the line is touching the current for the very first time in human history. We banish our knowledge that others assaulted the same stretch with equal vigour the previous day, and perhaps night. We see ourselves as pioneers.

By the time we return to the same pools later in the day, as we usually must, that sense of freshness and adventure has gone. We still believe that we *might* catch a fish. But few of us can contrive to summon up at 4 p.m. the True Believing spirit we possessed at 10 a.m., that we *will* catch a fish. Most rods are goaded to new exertions in the evening, on rivers where rotating beats change at 8 p.m. or 9 p.m. The belief that fresh fish must have come in since dinner, and that anyway our predecessors on the beat were duffers, provides a powerful incentive. This is especially true of the Helmsdale, where each night the bottom pools of the river, those adjoining marvels the Whinnie and the Marrel, are visited by post-prandial enthusiasts, eager to catch a fish heavy with sea lice, just in off the tide. When I get my own turn down there, I would camp overnight on the bank if I thought I could get away with it. On my final evening of salmon fishing last season, we had people to dinner at the lodge. After they went home, I reflected: at 8 p.m., we had inherited one of the most unpromising beats on the river. Ninety minutes remained until closing time. Everybody else thought I was mad, but I couldn't resist a cast. Not a fish moved, and the brief darkness was descending. I could scarcely glimpse my fly landing under the far bank. I came home empty-handed, and I am sure I was wasting my time. Angus the gillie would think it kindest to have me committed to some kind of home. Rationally, I am sure he is right. If one confined one's summer fishing to a few hours every morning, most of us could catch at least 70 per cent of the numbers we land after casting almost around the clock.

Yet it is different for him, because he lives on the river. For those of us restricted to occasional pilgrimages, the only way we know of fishing is to keep alive that glimmer of hope, and a fly on the water, even in the doggiest hours of the summer day. Here is my own favourite thesis about the whole business: over a period, as distinct from the chance of a single day or week, the man or woman who catches most fish will be he or she who has their rod on the water longest in good conditions. What counts most is not that the fisher should be a wizard, but that fish should be present and willing. Unfair, isn't it?

8

Hit and Miss

$\mathcal{W}$E ALL EMBRACE the red-letter days when, miraculously, everything goes right for us. When I am feeling down about sport, I lift my spirits by recalling an idyllic August outing a couple of years back. I shot quite straight. You may say: so what? That is because you shoot straight all the time. But for those of us who spend much of the season throwing lead about the sky with the promiscuity of a bridesmaid broadcasting confetti, an outing on which things really work is cause for trumpets, champagne and rejoicing within the bosom of the family as well in the gamebook.

That day, on a marvellous moor in the north of England, everything went right from the start. First, there was no rain. Anyone who wears spectacles knows that on a seriously wet day, he is doomed. For non-spectacle-wearers who wonder what the experience is like, try driving down the M4 in a thunderstorm without benefit of windscreen wipers. On this occasion, in perfect visibility I hit the first grouse that crossed me – always the start one wants. There was a wind just sharp enough to push the birds along a bit, without making them impossible. A bird flashed past my neighbour, who missed. I killed it behind. After that, a steady succession of grouse came at all angles. I hit some and missed some, but after a couple of drives I knew that I was shooting in a fashion that might not impress Percys or Strakers, but golly, it impressed me.

I made good practice at single birds and small coveys, even quite far out. I did much less well at packs. Try as one will, it is so hard to concentrate on one grouse among forty, to the exclusion of all the others. I recited aloud the familiar mantra 'Pick your bird, pick your bird,' every time I watched a cloud of brown bullets lifting over the heather towards me. Yet time after time, I fluffed them when they arrived. One sometimes came down, but seldom two. I killed a lot on my right in front, where I usually miss. Why? Because early in August I went to see Dylan Williams at the Royal Berkshire Shooting School. I fired 150 cartridges at his grouse layout. We quickly established that I was firing behind and above those right-handers. When it came to the real thing, I aimed ten feet in front and two feet below the grouse. Again and again, it fell. Everything is about believing that you know where to point the gun. I never understand why some people are reluctant to go back to school when their shooting goes wrong. How else can one raise one's game?

It is a terrific help to have somebody else in the butt, less for loading than for spotting. One pair of eyes can cover only so much of the horizon. Somebody saying, 'Right! Right!' at the critical moment makes all the difference. Frequently, Trevor my loader saw birds three or four seconds before I would have done. I had a bad drive in a burn bottom. A lot of grouse came high. They were not specially difficult, but they were completely different from the skimmers we had been shooting all morning. It is easy to become tuned to taking one sort of bird, then to be thrown when confronted by an unexpected one. We had a magical drive lining a ridge among rocks. The grouse kept coming, in ones, twos and small coveys. I wanted it never to end. When it was over, I picked up eighteen. My dog, who is seldom called upon to do that much work on my account, gazed at me in reproachful protest after retrieving eight. 'It's hot, and the pollen is something shocking,' he said. 'Can't we leave the rest for the pickers-up?'

By now, some readers are muttering in disgust: no wonder this spoilt booby managed to shoot a few grouse on an August day with two guns and clouds of birds. The case for the defence is that I walked-up game or shot over pointers for most of my life before I got a sniff of driven grouse. I dreamed for thirty years of the sort of day I am describing, before it came to pass. When it happened, I wanted to bottle it and slip it lovingly into the cellar, to console old age. 'I hope you know how lucky you are,' said my wife. You bet.

Afterwards, I rehearsed every detail in my mind, reflecting on what I could learn. Confidence, of course, is the vital ingredient. Once I started to hit birds consistently, I raised the gun with an assurance that is normally lacking. A bird flew past my neighbour and swung high behind the line. I gave it ten yards of lead, and fired when it was a good fifty yards out. It came down. I couldn't do as much again in a million years. Yet on a day when you believe in yourself, it is amazing what can happen.

It obviously makes a big difference to have plenty to shoot at – a good draw on a big day. Rough shooting, with half a dozen chances in a morning, is a much harsher test of a sportsman than a driven day on which one fires two hundred cartridges. August grouse-shooting flatters the guns. Birds fall down after being hit by a couple of pellets. In October, or even September, the same quarry a few weeks older laughs at you and flies on for miles. We cannot pretend that, on a still summer day, we saw the most challenging face of shooting. Yet how thrilled most of us are if such an outing gives us a chance to perform just a touch above our natural level, in a peerless mountain setting.

Two weeks after my tiny August triumph, on a September day in a stiff breeze, I was clambering up to the first line of butts on another moor, in Aberdeenshire. I will not go so far as to say that I was feeling cocky, but I was quietly confident. Aged fifty-seven, I was starting to think that I had cracked this grouse-shooting lark – well, quite, anyway. At the first drive, I was flank gun. Not a lot came over, but I did my best with the chances. I missed a couple, then got the distance and killed a long one on my left. There was a covey. I did not get a right-and-left, but killed two with one shot. A minute or two later, I hit another single bird behind. I had dispatched four birds for eight or nine cartridges, which is about as good as I do.

After that, however, mourners and wreaths were needed – not for the grouse, but for me. To be as honest as I can contrive, over the next two days each grouse that I killed required half a box of cartridges to send it to the pluckers. I sobbed and writhed, brooded and changed tactics, but strong men in neighbouring butts were having difficulty avoiding spontaneous combustions of laughter when they saw me raise a gun. I missed dozens coming straight at my butt. How can one fail to hit something, if one fires into ten grouse immediately in front? Yes, yes, I know the answer. Shooting into the brown never works, but that does not stop the foolish from trying.

The Reverend Sydney Smith observed two hundred years ago: 'The birds seem to consider the muzzle of my gun as their safest position.' So it was with me. I missed a lot almost overhead. I waited too long, sensed the blur of my shot in the air behind the birds, then compounded the folly by wasting the second barrel when the covey was five yards above my head. Somehow, I could not stop myself pressing the trigger, even when I was looking at empty air beyond the birds. When I did connect, it was always the single bird that fell. In two days, I could claim only a single right-and-left.

My neighbour was deadly. With quiet elegance, he pulled two birds out of a covey again and again. He wiped the eyes of us all at long birds behind. A fellow-gun said: 'He's been shooting grouse here since he was nine.' That might be true. But it is sobering constantly to be reminded that birds to which one is not bothering to raise a gun are, in reality, within range if the barrels look the right way. One will never kill grouse if one does not shoot at them.

In the stiff wind, which made every bird a thrill to watch, several coveys flew high down the line behind, and were missed by most of us. They were curling as well as motoring. I possess one useful talent as a shooter, which would qualify me to serve as a coroner at any game inquest: I can remember vividly afterwards what the birds did and where I put my gun, especially if I miss.

Years ago, I visited the Israeli army's commando school. One of the instructors said: 'You know what we mark most highly for? Telling the truth. So many disasters happen in battle because people are lost, bogged down, fail to reach their objectives and won't admit it. We say here: "If you always give us on the radio your exact situation and location, you will be forgiven almost anything."' This seems a good guide for life generally: whatever one's problem, it is necessary to confront it frankly. Thus, my gamebook represents an attempt honestly to assess my own performance, as well as my experience. Otherwise, I am committing the greatest folly of all, lying to the mirror.

Some people enjoy fibbing about their shooting prowess. After one Northumbrian grouse drive that I remember, when I admitted to only five birds down, somebody said: 'Johnny on your right says he had eighteen.' Now, the only thing that had consoled me in my frustration was the certainty that my neighbour was shooting worse; I didn't see Johnny touch a feather. But it cheered him to tell the world about his eighteen, even if it caused no end of bother for the pickers-up.

When the bag was counted at the end of our first day in Aberdeenshire, it proved to be twenty brace short of what we might have expected. Scent was poor. The dogs must have missed picking up a significant number of birds. As is often the case with grouse-shooting, the bag depended heavily on two proficient and experienced guns, admittedly aided by good draws. They must have accounted for around 40 per cent of our total. Quite a few others had performed — well, not much better than me. On our second day, the morning was slow. I had one delightful drive, standing in a flank butt on the top corner of a sheer two-hundred-foot hill. I was invisible to everybody else. Every opportunity was a snap shot. Only six or seven birds came my way, and I killed four. I walked down to lunch feeling that the splendour of the setting had inspired me to raise my game, together with being a touch more relaxed because no one else could see what I was doing.

The afternoon was magnificent, in every respect save my own marksmanship. On the dry hill, birds had concentrated where there was water. On our two last drives, coveys kept coming. The wind and the lie of the land caused an amazing number to fly down the line, offering themselves to four or five guns in succession.

Frequently, one had ten seconds or more to watch those wonderful brown shapes streak down the breeze in the fashion immortalised by Thorburn and Lodge, before the downturned wings zipped past, offering the sensation that excels all others in the eyes of almost every sporting gun. The gunmaker Robert Churchill used to suggest that one should shoot at a bird 'when it looks big enough to eat'. Some of the grouse I missed that September afternoon were big enough to count the feathers. My father wrote a couple of books with the promising titles *How to Shoot Straight* and *Why we Miss*. I took them down from the shelf that evening and browsed through a lot of stuff about footwork, lifting one's head from the butt, not taking second aim, and so on. I knew this was all perfectly sound, but none of it answered the question about why I had made a pig's ear of my day. I would guess that I was shooting underneath most of the birds I fired at, because I was raising the barrels of the gun more slowly than the stock. It has been my lifelong weakness to do everything, including shooting, in too much of a hurry.

Because I am so large, when birds have a good view I crouch in the butt, uncoiling myself at the last second. This causes lots of grouse to swing abruptly through ninety degrees, in a fashion a Spitfire pilot would have respected. Unkind people often demand post-mortems on grouse that die around me, to determine how many expired of mere shock on suddenly being confronted with two and a half yards of tweed at point-blank range. When I apologised to my host for doing less than justice to his birds, he said cheerfully: 'Don't worry about it. The great thing is that you enjoyed yourself.' This is, of course, the famously polite rejoinder to such observations. Yet in truth, unless one can command the sympathy due to a novice, any gun owes it to keepers, beaters, pickers-up and the moor to make a reasonable showing. Even on an 'off' day, grouse-shooting is irresistible. At the end of my anguished outing in Aberdeenshire, I told my neighbour truthfully that it had been a privilege to watch him shoot. But in one's heart, in such circumstances, how one yearns to give the next gun reason to say the same to oneself.

9

Love Affair With Labs

'YOU'RE SO LOVELY . . . Yes, yes . . . Go on . . . You're so clever . . . That's wonderful . . . Yes, yes, yes.' Relax. This is not an extract from a *Coronation Street* star's intimate memoirs, nor even from mine. It is the sort of speech that otherwise sensible men and women make every day to their labradors. Makes your toes curl, does it? You say that you never speak to Towser or Ponto like that? I don't believe you. All dogs make fools of their owners, and somehow labradors make bigger fools of us than any. We love and tickle them, scratch them and gossip to them with much less inhibition than we display before two-legged loved ones. The moment those soulful, melancholy eyes look up into ours, we melt. I have seen tycoons, whom it is wise during business hours to count one's fingers after shaking hands with, become marshmallows when addressing their labs. I have watched women who spit out husbands like cherry stones become wilting softies as the faithful old black beast trots up to present them with a pheasant.

A woman friend came home from shopping to find her husband lying on his back on the kitchen floor. She demanded: 'What's wrong with you?' He said: 'Absolutely nothing. I was just hoping to get you to give me the sort of welcome you give the four-letter dogs.' Last season, at a shoot on the Welsh Marches, I had a row with a woman picker-up whom I urged to go off and retrieve pheasants for one of the seven guns who did not have dogs with them. She remained defiant, and kept retrieving immediately behind me. We exchanged abuse. I found myself musing for the hundredth time about pickers-up who believe that the day is laid on for their dogs. A picker-up once said to me: 'It's our day out too, you know.' I asked: 'How much have you paid to be here?'

The interesting part of my confrontation in the Marches came afterwards. My host reported that this Boadicea had complained bitterly. I had sworn at her dog. Sworn at it? I came within a whisker of shooting it. Yet I suspect that Boadicea would have taken both barrels in her own bottom without a whimper. Her wrath was roused by the notion that anyone had dared to raise a voice to the apple of her eye, the lodestar of her life, the cream bun at her tea table – her Fido.

I am too conscious of the imperfections of my own dog team to get upset about fellow-guns' mockery of them. The Labrador Retriever Club of Great Britain warns us in its literature that the breed 'can be wilful if they sense they have the upper hand'. My old Paddy is now so wilful (and deaf) that after a drive he simply disappears into the nearest wood until he feels like coming back. I yearn to breed from one of the Hastings animals, but the aforesaid LRC of GB warns against inciting promiscuity: 'Experienced stud dogs look upon mating bitches as a routine part of their lives.' Makes them sound like Russell Crowe, doesn't it? However, 'a family pet dog, faced with the prospect of the very occasional mating, could become stressful and difficult to manage'. Tough luck, the young entry. I hope shooting continues to give you a big thrill, because other excitements are off the menu.

Seriously though, the dominance of black labradors among shooting men and women grows with each passing season. Everybody loves spaniels. It is a joy to see them well worked by an accomplished handler. But so few guns can manage them in the field. They need a master hand, all the year around. Most of us slobber over our dogs in the sitting room for eight months of the year, then expect them to behave like Guardsmen in the shooting season. Labradors, such wonderfully forgiving animals, are far more likely than spaniels to retain at least a semblance of discipline amid erratic emotional treatment.

I have a weakness for pointers and setters, and embrace any chance to watch them work over grouse. But I am not foolish enough to imagine that I could manage one. They need constant, extravagant exercise. I feel sorry for any pointer or setter that inhabits a home where it is simply turned out to run around the garden, however much love is lavished upon it. They are dogs for professionals. For the amateur, there is nothing to beat a lab. I like the smaller examples, and don't warm to those heavily-built beasts with big heads which win lots of field trials, with names that always seem to have Sandringham in them. I was watching a hefty labrador at work the other day, and knew that it reminded me of something. Yes, it was a Challenger tank that I had seen lurching over an assault course, flattening everything in its path. By contrast, the leggy, whippet look may not appeal to judges at Cruft's, but looks great on the stubble in December, coursing a runner.

The right question for any prospective dog owner is: what do you want it for? Some people intend a four-legged acquisition to make a statement about themselves. They want to tell the world that they are original thinkers. They will go to the ends of the earth to acquire brown labradors or Chesapeake retrievers or whatever. Who can forget poor Tuppy Glossop in P.G. Wodehouse's tale, who sacrificed all to find an Irish water spaniel for a doggy girl he had fallen in love with, only to see her run off with another specimen? That story has prejudiced me against the breed ever since. I am not saying that golden retrievers or brown labradors or poodles are a mistake in the shooting field – a legion of owners can prove me wrong. I simply suggest that, for the averagely incompetent handler (which, by definition, means most of us), the odds on success are better with a black lab, just as the chances of avoiding trouble with a motor car are greater if one opts for a family estate rather than a Maserati.

On the debit side, of course, at shoots one faces frequent embarrassment for shouting at, signalling to, and seizing pheasants from a dog that turns out to be somebody else's. There are so many black labradors at the average sporting occasion that I sometimes think of painting white stripes along the side of mine, to clarify the situation. But then old Paddy waddles arthritically back from the other side of the field, sobbing with pleasure about the bird clutched in his steel-trap jaws; or the young entry sits expectant beside me, looking like a perfectly behaved gun dog (so long as you don't notice his corkscrew). A surge of love and intimacy courses through the veins. Make you feel queasy, that sort of language? Only because it's not your black lab.

Many families have differences of opinion about what to call babies. These are as nothing, however, compared with the frenzied debates about what to call animals. Your children may eventually forgive you for giving them names like Zachariah or Cherie or Rollo, but there is nothing to beat the anguished embarrassment of a spaniel summoned across three fields by bellows of 'Lulu!' or 'Waffles!' or even 'Caesar!' Whenever we acquire a new dog, a lot of midnight oil gets burned as we try to work out what to call it. For years I enjoyed teasing lefties when naming dogs. One of the great things about politically correct people is that they will rise to a fly in a fashion that would make me a champion angler if fish were equally responsive.

Thus, in the early 1970s I christened my labrador Stokeley, after a notorious American black militant named Stokeley Carmichael. His successor, Tweedie, owed her name to the legendary *Guardian* feminist columnist, Jill Tweedie. I enjoyed the outrage this caused in liberal circles, but everybody else took pity on the dogs. Thereafter, we adopted a more romantic approach. Francie Fitzpatrick was an Irish spaniel who took her name from Somerville & Ross's most sympathetic heroine, though I should have remembered that the book in which she stars, *The Real Charlotte*, is a dark piece, in which Francie comes to a sad end. Our Francie was deeply lovable, but not much of a gun dog.

The older Hastings lab answered to Paddy when we got him from his breeder. I was superstitious enough not to change his name, because he seemed happy with it, and remains so to this day. What about the next one, however? I flirted with Argus, the name of Odysseus' dog, not least because, like me, his owner had a wife named Penelope. However, I was persuaded by wiser counsels that a) 'Argus!' sounds pretty silly when shouted at a dog busy wrecking the next drive, as any dog of mine probably will, and b) it is tactless to name an animal after one that dropped dead as soon as it saw its master.

Most of us either try to be original when we name our animals, or resort to expedients so hackneyed that one expects the poor beast concerned to die of shame. In the first category, I once met a poor dog named Cymbeline – he wasn't much of a retriever either. In the second, a few years ago there was an embarrassing period when, if you shouted 'Purdey!' at the average shoot, fourteen dogs would quickly be licking your face. Lord Kitchener, he of Khartoum, possessed four spaniels respectively christened Shoot, Bang, Miss and Damn. One meets legions of animals named Teal, Grouse or Wigeon. In the nineteenth century, if sporting writers of the period are to be believed, partridge stubbles were densely populated with pointers and setters called Ponto. In that classically educated age there was also a canine host of Hectors and Lysanders, and even Achilles.

Horses' names don't seem as important as those of dogs, perhaps because it never seems to do you much good to call a horse to heel or tell it to get off the sofa. Fences, oats and spurs play the chief part in motivating mounts, don't they? Equine names usually feature in conversation only in the third person: 'I've mucked out Squirrel,' or 'Will you tack up Bertie and take Black Beauty to the knackers?' I doubt whether Soapey Sponge ever muttered sweet nothings in Multum-in-Parvo's ear, though Siegfried Sassoon may have murmured a word to Cockbird going into the last fence of the Colonel's Cup. Wellington found Copenhagen an uncommonly serviceable vehicle, but I can't imagine the Duke wasting breath chatting to him on the ridge of Mont St Jean. And before the equestrian fraternity start writing me Disgusted of Newmarket letters, I had better admit to teasing you a trifle.

Cat-lovers assert that their beasts respond instantly to a name, but as a cat-sceptic I question whether even Hodge, the best-known cat in literature, took much notice of Dr Johnson unless there was something in it for him. Cats make investment bankers look unselfish. Indeed, even in the most madly feline households I notice that the beast in question is usually referred to simply as 'the cat', as in 'The cat's been sick again,' rather than as Orlando or Marmaduke or whatever.

Many of us use the names we give our animals to preserve an association that has meant a lot in our lives – a house, a mountain, even a river. My father called one of his spaniels Ruins, because the dog was born amid the broken stones of a Sussex castle. The Westminster family has always been able to call upon an almost limitless supply of their own properties after which to christen racehorses and dogs. The rest of us have to make do with other people's. The homeliest names often sound the most convincing – Charlies and Dollys and Sallys. How could those wretched Kennel Club stars hold up their heads, burdened all their manicured lives with birth certificates which declare them to be bounders like High Cross Mount Royal or St John Notting Hill or some such? Such creatures sound like confidence tricksters or Blair peers. Come to think of it, Falconer would make a good name for a slightly dodgy steeplechaser.

Children carry the homely approach to names to extremes. My son owns a hunt terrier named Trotter. Though normally an articulate young man, he is incapable of explaining where the handle came from. I blush to remember that nanny and I once had a budgerigar named Chirpy and a hamster named Hammy. I suppose you can argue that this hardly mattered, when those fine creatures were unlikely to have to be identified on a race card, or suffer their shame engraved on a large gold cup.

Only dogs' names really matter. Our latest family member has to put up with being a humdrum Stanley.

He complains that this makes him sound like a Bootle bank manager or the fall guy in a comedy double-act. I have explained to him that, while his is not a name many people nowadays give to their first-born, it is possessed of a special resonance in our household, because events in and around Port Stanley a generation ago have paid for much of the Hastings family's Pedigree Chum ever since. He has yomped triumphantly into the part.

For the nine years Paddy was the only dog in the Hastings ménage, his 'Wanted' notice when he went roaming, which was pretty often, ran like this: 'Male; labrador; hunting instinct – great; disciplinary ditto – less predictable; hormone count – high; mouth – of the Magimix persuasion; temperament – benign Piccadilly Highlander.' Hyde Park may not quite rival Inverness-shire in Paddy's affections, but he is untroubled by London or aeroplanes or long car journeys or, indeed by much except the vital three effs in a dog's life, of which two are food and pheasants.

Since Paddy entered old age, Stanley has taken up the torch. It is extraordinary to watch the behaviour of two animals of the same breed and some of the same bloodlines living under the same roof. We were nervous about how they would get on, but Paddy is astonishingly tolerant of Stanley, and Stanley is besotted with Paddy. If we try to move him without his old mate, he is horrified. I sometimes take Stanley for long bicycle walks, on the grounds that being younger, he needs more exercise. But every few hundred yards he stops and turns, looking for Paddy. My wife took the old dog to the vet the other day, to have one of his innumerable war wounds attended to, and to remortgage the house on the way to pay the bill. Stanley took two big gates like a steeplechaser in his efforts to follow the car.

There is no snarling, no fighting at the trough. If there is anything to be eaten, Paddy steps serenely to the front of the queue, sure of his status as top dog. Stanley waits patiently for Paddy to finish his coffee and liqueurs before essaying a mouthful. Then we come to looks. Paddy has many great qualities, but at no time could we have entered him as a page-three boy. Stanley, on the other hand, looks divine and knows it. Stanley thinks that looks will get him through life without any additional exertion. My wife believes occasional reluctance to tuck into his rations reflects delicacy about his figure. I don't suggest that he has ambitions on the catwalk, but maybe he believes there is a dogwalk. People who meet him in London parks feed his vanity by telling him how lovely he is, and asking whether we would like to mate him. No one considered Paddy as a possible sire for their bitch, if a polar bear was available as an alternative.

I took Stanley out for the odd day at the end of the first season he was with us. He picked up impeccably whenever he could see the bird. But if a runner disappeared into brambles, he stopped dead on the edge and turned to me like a petulant tennis star questioning a line call. 'You can't seriously expect anyone to scratch their nail varnish going through that lot?' he demanded. Yes, I know one is not supposed to let young dogs chase runners, but I wanted to see what happened.

I have never taken the two dogs out together, because it seems better to work Stanley on his own. I am fearful that when I do, the young dog will just stand there when a bird drops, looking at Paddy and waiting for him to do the work. Stanley certainly has a more sensitive mouth. The other day he found a pheasant egg, and presented it to us unbroken with a delicacy that touched our hearts. Paddy would have whisked up an omelette and devoured it without breaking stride.

I worry about Stanley's attachment to toys. A keen gun-dog-owner friend said: 'Oh, come on – he's young. Of course he likes toys.' But Stanley's devotion to carrying around fluffy stuffed animals seems somehow – you know, not terribly virile. We don't want him getting like Linus with his blanket in the Peanuts strip. Stanley runs like the wind. It is a joy to watch his long legs tearing up the grass. But I am not sure he has Paddy's guts. From the first day we had the old boy, he would drive headlong into any sort of cover after a bird. Stanley displays a vulnerable disposition. He cowers at a cross word, though he has been mollycoddled since the day we had him. Harry, his trainer, says he's sure the dog will gain confidence as he gets a bit older and has a bit more experience. I have told him (the pupil, not the trainer) that our house runs on the no pheasant, no food principle.

My wife, who adores Stanley, mutters that she will go on feeding him whether he retrieves birds or not. But what is one to make of a dog who sometimes jumps into the back of the car, but on other days sits below the tailgate, looking pleadingly up at Paddy, until one of us lifts him in or bribes him with a chocolate biscuit? By now, I fancy every serious dog owner among my readers is bridling with rage at the innumerable handling errors I have confessed. In mitigation, I would plead that at least we don't let dogs upstairs. But then this morning when the dogs thought I was away, I was appalled to hear scuffling at the bedroom door. After suitable reprimands had been issued and the culprits sent packing, I asked my wife whether she ever let Paddy and Stanley into the bedroom. She looked shifty. So did the dogs.

Thus there is a boudoir conspiracy to love Stanley, whether or not he does the job for which he is being fed. What would Gordon Brown say, I asked both wife and dog severely, if confronted with this flagrant breach of Welfare to Work principles? I can see a future stretching ahead in which poor arthritic old Paddy has to go on staggering across the moor finding grouse, while the beautiful Stanley lies ornamentally on the grass beside the 4 × 4, earning a fortune as an extra in motoring ads. I said to my wife: 'I don't think we've gained a gun dog. We're simply acting as stylists to a supermodel.'

10

A Future for the Countryside

Abridged from a lecture given in 2004 to members of the Campaign to Protect Rural England

Throughout our lifetimes, despite all the protestations of the British public about its love of the land, tensions have grown between town and countryside, as the urban and suburban majority asserts its power. It is dismaying how little most people know, about the simplest realities of what makes the countryside tick. Almost seventy years ago, in his novel *Scoop* Evelyn Waugh satirised the townsman's view, in his portrait of an executive of Lord Copper's ghastly *Daily Beast* newspaper:

> If a psychoanalyst, testing his associations, had suddenly said to Mr Salter the word 'farm', the surprising response would have been 'bang', for he had once between blown up and buried while sheltering in a farm in Flanders. It was his single intimate association with the soil. It had left him with the obstinate though admittedly irrational belief that agriculture was some-

thing alien and highly dangerous. Normal life, as he saw it, consisted in regular journeys by electric train, monthly cheques, communal amusements and a cosy horizon of slates and chimneys; there was something unEnglish and not right about 'the country' with its solitude and self-sufficiency, its bloody recreations, its darkness and silence and sudden, inexplicable noises; the kind of place where you never know from one minute to the next that you might not be tossed by a bull or pitch-forked by a yokel or rolled over and broken up by a pack of hounds.

My point here is that seventy years ago many townsmen were no more sympathetic to the countryside and its inhabitants than they are today. In the interval, however, two important things have changed. First, in the era of Evelyn Waugh's Mr Salter, city-dwellers displayed no ambition to impose their values upon the countryside. Today, by contrast, a moral conceit has evolved among the urban majority, reflected by the Labour Party in the House of Commons, that New Britain has a right, even a duty, to impose upon us all the values of a suburban monoculture. This conceit is vividly reflected in the legislative ban on fox-hunting, and also in draconian changes to planning legislation, which threaten vast areas of countryside with development, while tolerating only token county or local consultation about the descent of the bulldozers. Simon Jenkins, that trenchant columnist and crusader for our heritage, said recently that he does not believe the British people perceive the enormity of what the present government has done and is doing to the countryside. It is doubtful whether we have ever been ruled by people less sensitive to the welfare of the rural landscape.

At the heart of the new mood of urban interventionism is the fact that the old rural economic power, founded upon the importance of food production, has gone forever. This, in turn, has prompted the loss of agricultural political influence. The most important profit-making activities in today's countryside relate to leisure, amenity and tourism. Most money spent in the countryside is earned in cities. This does not mean that agriculture is no longer important. Most land will and must continue to be tilled. But the manner of that tillage, especially on poorer land, will increasingly be influenced by environmental and social considerations rather than by the old imperative of maximising production.

We are bound to be saddened by the social consequences of one agricultural revolution. Most farmers are shifting responsibility for cultivating their land to outside contractors. This is economically inevitable, because only the largest farms can support the capital burden of owning heavy machinery. In a few years, most traditional labour on farms big and small will be in the hands of regional contractors. All around us we see men driving huge machines who have no reason to care about pulping verges or the abuse of land on which they are mere birds of passage, rather than permanent stewards. We cannot welcome a future in which the vast majority of people working the soil have no personal stake in it. The trend seems inescapable, and it represents another blow to traditional patterns of community in rural life.

As the number of people engaged in agriculture continues to decline, the ethos of the countryside is increasingly influenced by incomers. The scale of social movement is astonishing. Between 1981 and 2002 the rural population of Britain grew by 1.7 million, or 13.7 per cent. There is estimated to be a net annual migration from cities and suburbs into the countryside of well over 100,000 people. Many of the arrivals are parents aged between twenty-five and forty-four, seeking a lifestyle for their children. The only age group still moving from the country to the cities is, unsurprisingly, that of sixteen- to twenty-four-year-olds, who find rural housing expensive and country life – as they always did – uncool.

One of the challenges for those of us who cherish the countryside is not to dissuade newcomers from joining us, but to urge them to be a little more modest about bringing into rural areas a baggage of urban and suburban expectations. It is sometimes a sad business, to see incomers arrive in villages and hamlets armed with the lifestyle convictions of the urban communities from which they have come, rather than with a willingness to adapt to those of the world they have chosen to join. My father used to remark with relish that the chief activities of the countryside are death and sex. Everyone with a little knowledge of wildlife knows this to be true. Yet today we see legal actions brought by people who object to the racket made by crowing cockerels, the rise of vegetarianism and so-called animal rights, and a recent opinion poll which showed that 29 per cent of respondents would support a ban on sport fishing, because they consider it cruel. A Hampshire farmer calculated recently that each year he removes from his land thirty-six tons of rubbish deposited by the public, most of them no doubt people who tell opinion pollsters how much they love nature.

Thoughtful country-dwellers would agree, I think, that while rural communities should enjoy as many amenities as possible, our aim should be to intrude as little as possible upon the natural order of things. It is dismaying to see kerbs and pavements springing up on country roads, railings erected around village ponds, white lines painted on modest byways, and a plague of unnecessary, grotesquely prominent advertising hoardings and signs. Most of the latter are erected in the name of public safety, an increasing preoccupation of our litigious society, the world of the blame culture. Yet each one diminishes the wildness and thus the beauty of the countryside. Who needs huge painted steel proclamations reading 'Welcome to Northamptonshire, Rose of the Shires', or 'Royal Berkshire: 50 years of Service to the Community'? This is expensive, meaningless tosh. There should be a presumption against every intrusion of this kind, unless a case can be made for its utility. There should always be a prejudice in favour of nature.

Even in the remotest areas of Britain, never mind in the Home Counties, an orange glow suffuses the night sky. Many villages now boast lighting which is wildly inappropriate to their character. We must acknowledge that the introduction of illumination often reflects the wishes of local people – though I suspect many of the enthusiasts are not country-born. But it seems as important that future generations should be able to behold the stars at night, as that they should enjoy the opportunity to see birds and wildflowers by day. The Campaign to Protect Rural England is proposing not that lighting should be removed, which would be absurd, but that it should be installed more sensitively, to illuminate the ground beneath, rather than to pollute the sky above. This is technically easy, by fitting shielded bulbs. It simply requires a recognition by local authorities, and ultimately by the public, of the damage done to a landscape by introducing excessive artificial light where there should be a prejudice in favour of minimising it.

It is the fact that any of us can live in a village and commute each day to a place of work forty, fifty, even a hundred miles distant that has changed the nature of the countryside, and rendered it so vulnerable. There is an apparently insatiable demand by English people to live in rural areas, which it is the business of property developers to convince governments must be satisfied at will. By contrast, it is the business of those of us who love the landscape to argue the case not against development, but against uncontrolled development. Unlimited, inadequately planned housing growth must mean the destruction of the very thing so many people profess to love.

The numbers about what is happening around us are frightening. On current trends, by 2021 there will be almost four million more households in Britain than there are today, chiefly because so many of us dislike our families too much to want to live with them. In the course of the twentieth century, average household size almost halved, from 4.6 to 2.4 people. The number of one-person households increased from two million in 1961 to nearly eight million in 2000. Almost three-quarters of the increase in households over the next twenty years will be accounted for by people wanting to live alone. If such statistics sound wearisome, it is necessary to grasp the magnitude of the problem we face if the government is prepared to allow unlimited development on greenfield sites to meet the alleged demand for all those new households.

What renders the countryside so special is that no more of it can be made. Each time a small piece of England is built upon, it disappears forever. The government's Countryside Agency recently published a document entitled *The State of the Countryside 2004*. Seldom has a more dismaying volume of Third-Way waffle and sociologist-speak issued from Whitehall. I will quote at random a sample of its language about 'countryside change':

We have sought to build a robust and neutral indicator that will stimulate a wide debate about the general concept. In reporting changes that are consistent or inconsistent with general character, we do not imply that these changes are 'good' or 'bad' or that the existing character of the countryside charac-

ter ought to be preserved. Rather, we seek to high-
light how contemporary change relates to our current
understanding of countryside character, and allow
stakeholders at all levels to explore the significance
of these changes.

Wonderful, is it not, to contemplate how Mr Badger and
Tess of the d'Urbervilles, or for that matter John Jorrocks,
would have reacted to hearing themselves described as
'rural stakeholders'? The document goes on:

> The availability of the present indicator ... rep-
> resents a major step towards the realisation of these
> aims and should help to maintain the rich diversity
> and distinctiveness of the English countryside.

There are a further 294 pages of this stuff, and if you can
make head or tail of it, you are a better man than I am,
Gunga Din.

There is a serious point here. What seems most frightening about the utterances emanating from government
over recent years concerning rural development is that,
beneath a torrent of verbiage and protestations of good
intentions, they are surrender documents – deeds of
capitulation as absolute as any defeated army has signed
at the conclusion of a war. The relevant Whitehall depart-
ments and their agencies appear to have concluded that
pressures for housing development in the English countryside are greater than the government is willing or able to
resist. The government has accepted a prediction that over
the next sixteen years 4.2 million new homes must be built

in England. An area as large as today's greater London threatens to disappear under building in the south-east alone.

THE BRITISH CHARACTER.
DETERMINATION NOT TO PRESERVE THE RURAL AMENITIES.

It was ever thus: a Pont cartoon for Punch,
published in 1935

Alun Michael, the Rural Affairs Minister, said in an interview recently: 'We don't want rural Britain to become a museum of the landscape. Planning rules must make rural communities fit for the twenty-first century.' What this means, in practical terms, is that a historic presumption in favour of the traditional county development plan has now been replaced by centrally directed growth and targets to accelerate the planning process. In March 2004 Gordon Brown declared his support in principle for Ms Kate Barker's report for the Treasury, of which the main conclusion was that housing should be made more affordable by building so much of it across the countryside that prices fall in a flooded market. She has argued that planning constraints are a malign force in preventing builders from creating as much housing as is needed to meet the alleged shortage of dwellings in Britain.

This seems an almost insane vision of economic engineering, an experiment whose consequence would be a floodtide of building to achieve its stated aim. If Barker's proposal is implemented, it will provoke the most reckless invasion of the rural environment conducted by any government in history. It pursues a strategy founded upon a cardinal error, that of regarding housing as a mere commodity, the supply of which can be adjusted at will, like output of motor cars or computers, without heed to the historic consequences for our fragile environment.

One of CPRE's most important recent pieces of research was commissioned from Europe Economics, following the Barker Report. EE studied Barker's data, and concluded that almost all its underlying assumptions were simply wrong. First, it is not true that there is a desperate shortage of roofs in this country. Between 1991 and 2001 the number of households in Britain grew by 1.2 million. Yet during this same period, 1.5 million new dwellings were created. Second, Barker, the Treasury and the Deputy Prime Minister insist that a shortage of land for building is driving up house prices, and use this argument to justify the dismantling of planning safeguards. Yet Europe Economics point out that in such countries as America and

Australia, where virtually unlimited land is available for building, prices have risen in recent times just as ours have, driven by the same factors – speculation and low interest rates, not shortage of land. CPRE is also deeply concerned about the government's apparent willingness to permit the invasion of Green Belt, a simple and extraordinarily effective planning device which has served Britain well for decades. Green Belt needs some imaginative updating, but this should relate to how it is regulated and managed, not to its scope. A further critical issue is that far too many development proposals ignore the need for supporting services and natural resources – above all water.

Late in 2004 we received important help in resisting Barker from an unexpected quarter. Her report asserted blithely that it was not her job to assess the environmental implications of her million-house top-up plan. Researchers at the Department of Food and Rural Affairs produced their own study, however, which sent shockwaves through Whitehall. Implementing Barker, they concluded, would require concreting 192,000 acres of greenfield land, an area half the size of Buckinghamshire, in addition to all possible brownfield sites. The pollution and environmental impact would be devastating.

Yet none of these arguments has so far sufficed to dissuade government from making bulldozers its apparent weapons of choice for imposing a cruel stamp upon rural England. It appears to share the impatience once expressed by one of Noël Coward's characters about 'all that unnecessary countryside'. Whitehall now has a right to overrule what it perceives as mere parochial interests resisting development, if it perceives 'a wider benefit to society at large'. We all know that nobody's loyalties in rural England are or ever will be to some nebulous region. They are to our counties. We think of ourselves, and always will, as belonging to Northamptonshire or Leicestershire, Wiltshire or Cornwall. Yet despite the defeat of the Deputy Prime Minister's 2004 referendum on the proposal for the first elected regional assembly, these bodies today possess most of the real power over English planning decisions, and are answerable only to John Prescott. Much of CPRE's most important work involves giving expert evidence on planning proposals, and contesting those which seem misguided, in a fashion which no other body does. Today, those questioning or contesting planning proposals find themselves obliged, willy-nilly, to go to a regional assembly's planning department to fight the cause of the countryside, because that is where government has vested power. It would be naïve to suggest that the misbegotten policy can readily be undone, but this should be our objective. No one should doubt that local democracy is set at naught by the current distribution of planning powers.

Almost the public's only means of thwarting government development plans now lie in the so-called consultative process. This makes CPRE's function in mobilising opinion critically important. We need to persuade more people to write letters, turn out for meetings, show politicians in the clearest terms what is and is not acceptable to communities.

We should be especially dismayed by the government's indifference to what we might call 'ordinary' countryside

– that is to say, landscape that is neither designated of outstanding natural beauty, nor of special scientific interest, yet which means a great deal to the people who live in its midst. The fear is that such landscape will be deemed to deserve no protection, and will thus be perceived by builders as 'up for grabs'. What we need from government, and what is today absent, is recognition that the entire countryside is the most precious natural resource this overcrowded island possesses.

John Prescott appears to focus his concerns upon national parks. These are perfectly acceptable as model estates, leisure centres – call them what you will. But if our children and grandchildren are to depend solely upon specimen relics of rural life to know what the English countryside means, then the future will be sterile. Our business is with England as a whole, with the warp and woof and county identities of the landscape, with a rural existence which is not something to be visited on a school tour, a bank holiday or July walking tour, but lived in 365 days a year.

What does 'protecting the English countryside' mean? We can all agree upon a vision of a green landscape which harbours the traditional flora and fauna. But throughout its history that landscape has always been changing, and so have the people who live in it. Economic forces have influenced the way that England looks, sometimes for good and sometimes for ill, since the beginning of time. We cannot pickle the countryside, even if we wanted to do so. There is no future in nostalgia. Many 'traditional country people' who knew, say, East Anglia seventy years ago, would argue that it is today a significantly better place to live in than it was then, even if it has abandoned all those picturesque outside loos, night carts and a pre-occupation with incest. In assessing rural development we must be receptive– for instance – to the need for change of use of redundant agricultural buildings. We should acknowledge a good case for light industries in villages. These offer local sources of revenue generation, and replace the lost blacksmiths, wheelwrights, millers, carters who were essential parts of any dynamic community a century or two ago. A village composed solely of residential housing can be quite as sterile as an industrial estate. The right mix is vital.

If we campaigned against all building, we would deserve dismissal as fantasists. Some greenfield development is inevitable, though tremendous scope remains for maximising housing on brownfield sites in urban and suburban areas, and for higher densities of building. Where development is proposed, our task is to ensure that a reasoned case must be always made for it. To identify proposals and threats in a given area, the community's first line of defence must be the local busybodies – yes, the Nimbys. In recent years, the word Nimby – Not In My Backyard – has been given a pejorative meaning by housebuilders and politicians whom local democracy does not suit.

The most frequent charge thrown by ministers and housing lobbyists against people like me – and perhaps like you – is that we are selfish snobs who, having secured our own little slice of rural heaven, are now fighting to

deny this to others. It is striking that whenever New
Labour runs out of rational arguments to support a policy,
it falls back upon hurling a charge of 'snobbery' against
its critics. To most of us, it seems absolutely natural and
right that local people should have a voice in what is done
to their own community. Instead of branding protesters
against philistine developments as Nimbys, such local
heroes deserve applause as crusaders, people prepared to
stand up and ask questions about plans thrust upon them
by remote regional authorities, or by ministers far away
in Whitehall who would not recognise a cuckoo if it laid
an egg in their gin and tonic. Local busybodies are often
the most useful and valuable members of their community, in contrast to those unwilling to notice, never
mind act against, monstrous developments imposed by
ministerial fiat.

Yet if it is easy to agree about the importance of obliging
government to consult with local communities, the other
force in all rural development is, of course, the people
who own the land. Those of us who live in the countryside
while not deriving our income from it should display
some humility towards those who do. That does not mean
nodding through every building proposal, but rather
recognising the imperatives landowners face. A large
number, perceiving a decline of agricultural incomes
which is almost certainly irreversible, see development as
the only way to make money from land. It is much more
profitable to grow concrete than corn. High-quality farm-
land, especially in East Anglia, will continue to provide
good incomes from high-intensity crops, even without
subsidy. Other farmers in less favoured areas cannot do

so. Farmers may not want to be park keepers, but an element of this is essential for their future, and for ours. We must, however, expect to pay them to do the job.

Some people suggest that small farming is inherently better for us all than big farming. There is no environmental evidence for this. If anything, the reverse is true. We all want to see small units survive. But those who own them will have to rely upon other sources of income for their livelihoods, as do small farmers on the Continent. It may prove a blessing, rather than the curse some critics suggest, if the next few decades see an expansion of hobby-farming by people who buy land because they love it and are interested in managing it for beauty and wildlife, rather than because they need or expect to make money from it.

Even though some of us are in the business of resisting unrestricted development, it would be naïve, even impertinent, to ignore the importance of the economic issue. To put it in the simplest terms, if as a society we want land to be cultivated or stewarded as an amenity for our pleasure, rather than exploited for development or ruthlessly intensive cultivation, we must be prepared to pay the cash price for this privilege. The hardest lesson of all about the countryside is that saving it will cost money, a lot of public money. It would be foolish to suggest that today, government or the public accept this, at either macro or micro level.

To give a micro example: a friend of mine owns an estate on the edge of a northern conurbation. A year or two ago he approached some local riding stables with a proposal that he would open and maintain riding routes all round the estate in return for a very modest annual subscription from riders who use it. I said that this sounded a marvellous initiative, which should be widely encouraged. He told me that, to a man and woman, the local horsey community rejected his proposal. They prefer to ride free along roads, rather than pay anything to exercise amid green spaces. This seems a tiny illustration of the steep hill we must climb to persuade the British people that the countryside is not, and never can be, free. It costs a huge amount of money, and somebody is going to have to pay. In the past, agricultural subsidy did the business, though that was not its purpose. As long as the taxpayer was generously underwriting farmers' lifestyles, it was not unreasonable for him to expect them to provide some amenity stewardship in return. Today, by contrast, Right to Roam legislation has been thrust upon the landowning community at the very moment when support from the taxpayer is being drastically reduced. If nobody is willing to pay landowners to look after the countryside for us, if farm incomes stay flat and other sources of cash cannot be found, we shall all be losers. Desperate landowners will adopt any recourse to save their skins – housing, airport extensions, industry, wind farms.

For all their professions of concern for the countryside, a depressing number of people are willing to sit on their hands while it vanishes. In this sense the present government is making a shrewd calculation, that it can afford to maintain essentially philistine rural policies because to do so will not cost many votes. Our job is to convince them otherwise; to make a noise, to cry from the rooftops the folly of destroying tracts of rural Britain that can never be replaced, to rouse people's anger about what is being taken from them, above all through the abolition of local and county planning rights.

Why is it that so many people who live in the country-side show no interest in looking after it? Inertia stems partly, I think, from a widespread belief that rural Britain is simply something that exists, independent of human agency. We must spread the message that this is mistaken. The countryside – even, or especially, including its wilder-nesses – is in not in a state of nature. It requires constant, expensive management. We cannot leave this to God and government. Good landowners are entitled to be proud of their stewardship, their long-term dedication to tree-planting, wildlife, woodlands and streams. The public, which once loved and respected Farmer Giles, is now bitterly sceptical about him because of past environmental follies, many of which should properly be blamed on government. The key to success for every organisation devoted to protecting the rural environment is that we should be perceived not merely as 'no' people, forever resisting development, but also as 'yes' people, possessing a vision for the future of the English countryside as a whole which catches the imagination of those who share our hopes as well as our fears.

Each time I walk the Wiltshire Downs or the North-umbrian hills, the Kennet Valley or the East Anglian coast-line, I marvel, as we all do, at how much natural beauty survives to fight for. There is no one-fits-all answer to the problems of the countryside, as government sometimes seems to suppose. Each region possesses its own character, advantages and difficulties. England, its agriculture and rural economy, is a patchwork. Preserving the diversity of its landscape as well as its fauna must be our objective. It has changed, is changing and will continue to change, amid the huge range of economic and social pressures which bear upon it. Any campaigning body that wishes to be taken seriously must adopt a dynamic vision, rather than a static one.

It is sometimes said that all that is needed for tyrants to flourish is for good men and women to do nothing. In the same vein, all that is needed to enable careless politicians and greedy developers to despoil our shrinking rural heritage is for the rest of us to stand by in silence. It is frightening how many people seem willing to do just that. Politicians are seldom long-term thinkers. Few ministers of any party hue are willing to contemplate a future that stretches further than the next election. Many, indeed, cannot bring themselves to think beyond next week. It can be frightening to see how readily they commit themselves to policies that will have a dramatic impact upon the lives of us all in twenty or thirty years. They do so because they know that they themselves will be long gone from office before these policies come to fruition. The outcome doesn't matter – to them.

There could not be a greater contrast between the short-termism of politicians and the long view adopted by such an organisation as CPRE. Our common task is to think not merely years, but decades ahead, to secure our heritage of green places and open spaces for future generations. All current Whitehall forecasts for the countryside appear to be based upon worst-case scenarios about housing need, together with a belief that mere aesthetics cannot be allowed to interfere with the sacred good of economic growth. In truth, of course, the future must lie in striking a balance which acknowledges the need for rural Britain to earn its living and find room for more people, without destroying the natural joys which draw millions who want to share them. The Campaign to Protect Rural England is committed not to resisting all change, but to managing it sensitively and imaginatively for our children and grandchildren. This seems a worthy purpose. It is a sadness that so many people seem content to remain spectators, while the bulldozers grind remorselessly onward. Surely the most important duty of anyone who claims to love the countryside is to join the battle for its future, if only by supporting the organisations which are fighting on behalf of us all.

11

No Eye for a Horse

CANTERING ACROSS THE Argentine pampas the other day in my impeccably polished Lobb jodhpur boots, I was thinking about my relationship with horses. Oh, hang on a minute. Perhaps I should qualify each of those clauses before we continue. I was clinging to the saddle in the lather of fear inseparable from any riding expedition of mine. The Lobb boots were made for me in a moment of financial madness thirty years ago – I had to increase the mortgage on my flat to pay for them. And we should acknowledge that all my life I have had a better chance of understanding a conversation in Malay dialect than getting on intimate terms with a quadruped.

Now, don't misunderstand. I am not in the least equiphobic, to coin a word. Indeed, I have always been madly jealous of those who can manage a horse well, whether hack or hunter. I accept the late Colonel Harry Llewellyn's view that 'The outside of a horse is good for the inside of a man.' But just as some of us find it difficult to empathise with computers or bond with golfers, so I have never learned how to talk to a horse in a fashion likely to persuade it to do what I want.

My riding career began circa 1950, trotting round the indoor school of a certain Major Glover at Chieveley in west Berkshire on a pony named Ginger. Major Glover was one of the great regiment of retired cavalry officers who taught riding to my generation. His clipped phrases and the twitches of his highly disciplined black moustache announced unmistakably how unlikely we were to qualify for a half-decent mounted unit. Jorrocks remarked on a man who preferred aspersions to be cast on his morals than on his 'hossmanship'. I abandoned any pretensions to the latter at the age of about seven.

I liked the lessons well enough, but never went home complaining that Daddy would not give me a pony. I would have preferred, say, a ray gun or an ice axe. I only began to enjoy ponies during a spell in my early teens when I used to ride across the Downs with a pair of local brothers who were wild as hawks but managed horses brilliantly. I rode a beast of theirs named Coco, which I sometimes thought myself in control of. We loved long treks along chalk tracks criss-crossing the Ridgeway, where in those days one hardly saw a soul, and certainly no horrible off-roaders. For a while, I was keen enough to attend a few local horse trials, to turn out for Badminton and local point-to-points.

Part of me wanted to be horsey because horses were so much a part of the country world in which I sought to live. How I would have adored to emulate Siegfried Sassoon, winning his race on Cockbird in *Memoirs of a Fox-hunting Man*, or for that matter to ride in the Grand National.

Yet then as now, it was hard to get into the whole horse thing seriously unless one's family was committed. My parents rode occasionally. My father owned more kit than Gordon Richards, but I would not have trusted him to bridle a hunter right way forward. Whatever our rural pretensions, in truth we were weekenders.

My only hunting outing in those days took place while I was at Oxford. Driving back from Bicester one afternoon, I met a friend out with the Drag. 'Look, Max,' he said, 'I need to get home in a hurry. Can I take your car, and you take my horse?' I jumped a few fences and lived to tell the tale, but my tweed suit went down badly with

the Master. Then I married into a serious hunting family, and learned how little I knew about horses. I have never forgotten the horror that greeted my first, innocent suggestion that it might be nice to go for a hack on a brilliant June morning: 'People don't *ride* in the *summer*.' OK, so I learned my lesson on that one, and a good deal more besides. I never felt at home at meets or as a foot follower, but I shared an enduring swell of pride to see one of my family beautifully turned-out on a hunter or, in the case of my children, taking jumps at a gymkhana, whacking hell out of a ball at Pony Club polo. The beauty of horses is irresistible even if one is incapable of judging or managing one.

Racecourses seem the least attractive places to see horses at their best, however. In such settings the magic of the animal is tarnished, in my eyes at least, by the seediness inseparable from any gambling sport. A cousin of mine who owned racehorses surprised me one day by remarking that he never placed a bet. 'I'm afraid I know too much about how it's done,' he explained sardonically. A racing friend, in every other respect a man of unimpeachable integrity, expressed outrage when Lester Piggott was jailed after his troubles with the taxman. 'Don't they understand?' he demanded. 'You can't send *Lester* to *prison*. What he's done is just the way racing is.' Yes, well, speaking as a non-racing man ... For a brief spell, however, we owned a stake in a steeplechaser that won a race at Wexford at 13–1. The Irish racing game took on a certain charm, before expiring a lot of bills and several losing races later. I knew how Christopher Fildes felt when he wrote his incomparable essay about owning losers: 'When friends want to know how my horse is or what he is doing, in my bleaker moods, I say that he has taken a one-way ticket to Melton Mowbray, home of the pie-making industry. All I still have, on my race-glasses, is an out-of-date badge from Salisbury saying "Owner". This year instead of a horse I am paying for a builder.'

I still enjoy riding holidays in Africa and South

America, where one treats a horse simply as a means of locomotion. There is no better way to see country or wild animals than from a saddle, and no need to advance faster than a trot. An advantage of middle age is that one no longer cares about being thought wet for jogging sedately across the bush and declining to join a burn-up party. A safari guide observed politely last year that she would not describe me as 'riding fit'. I never was, dear woman, I never was. I retain a deep unease about unpredictable equine behaviour, which seems supported by the evidence of the number of riders who bear the scars. 'Horses are fine until they are not fine,' in the wise words of my old friend, and devoted fox-hunter, Michael Sissons.

We don't have horses at home any more. I miss the sights and sounds and scents of the stable: the scraping of hooves on cobbles, a grazing mare in the field, the rich leather and gleaming steel of impeccable tack. On the other hand, though I never did much mucking out, I have always believed that the only happy horse-owner over the age of sixteen is one with somebody else doing the dirty work. I have occasionally stayed in houses where one is simply handed the reins and told to climb aboard. Those are the places where I feel I could become really keen.

Once I'm in the saddle, however, my problems become more serious. To place-drop for a moment, I once rode a pony in Ethiopia which, as I realised on seeing photographs afterwards, was smaller than me. In general, because I am so large, people put me on very big horses, which I am incapable of controlling. I once galloped for twenty minutes in circles round Skeffington Vale on a hunting day. Being unable to stop the great borrowed beast, I could only jam its rudder hard to starboard. The horse and I eventually resolved our differences by parting company.

When we lived in Ireland, the McCalmonts at Mount Juliet mounted me a few times, chiefly for the comic value of watching what happened. I adored the experience, as I have enjoyed each of my odd hunting forays. But the gulf has proved unbridgeable between my yearning to see the action at the front and my inability to sit a horse well enough to stay the distance. In the end, after a back operation a few years ago, I admitted defeat and acknowledged that after fifty, following hounds is too dangerous for anyone as incompetent as I am. I shall always love to see and hear horses. I feel as stricken as any Quorn follower by the hunting ban. But I have been forced to recognise that I am a natural footling, not an equestrian. More's the pity, those old Lobb boots are the only things about me that will ever look the part in stirrups.

12

Poachers' Roles

$\mathscr{I}$T IS A nice question whether the best arbitrators of behaviour are perfect gentlemen who have never hit a woman without first removing their hats, or cads and bounders who have committed every known social crime. I rather fear that in the sporting field I can claim a certain expertise, because I have been guilty of more lapses than most. The other day at a busy partridge drive, I found myself out of the shooting. At last, a bird headed towards me. I raised the gun. Thirty yards out the partridge swerved aside, heading two pegs from me. Cross and thwarted, I took a poke anyway – and missed as I deserved. The bird was killed down the line. I ended up feeling both foolish and unsporting. Many of us do things like that from time to time. We hope no one has noticed, though of course they do. Poaching from one's neighbour at driven shoots is probably the commonest vice and thus the most boring.

Most of us, when we are young and green, commit solecisms because we don't know any better. In my twenties and even thirties, a day's driven shooting was enough of an event to make me nervous. I did not get enough practice confidently to judge the nuances of how to behave with the assurance of a shoot owner's son who was out two days a week. As guns get older, however, we have fewer excuses for error. That does not save us from excitement and excess. We have all read stories about how a covey of eight grouse flew between Lords Walsingham and de Grey. They killed the lot, because each gun perfectly understood which birds properly belonged to him. I'm not sure I believe this yarn, because the men concerned were legends for sporting greed, as well as prowess. More to the point, at a lot of shoots it is simply not possible to be sure who should fire at a bird.

There are drives at which pegs are placed only twenty yards apart. When two guns are that close, how can any of us judge who has a better claim? Diffident and perfectly mannered guns call 'Yours,' if in doubt. Some of us, however, have trouble being diffident and perfectly mannered all the time. Another twist is that one often finds oneself on a peg at which a bird coming straight forward offers a less sporting target than it does to the next gun. Nobody except the most tiresome martinet can mind a neighbour taking the better shot. Likewise, at very high bird shoots in Devon or Yorkshire, local rules support the view that whichever gun thinks he can take a shot at a pheasant should do so. By the time you have examined the niceties of who is directly underneath some oxygen-breathing superbird half a mile up, it is over the next valley.

It is a long-established mark of prowess to wipe a man's eye by shooting the bird he has missed. Embarrass-ment sets in only when a neighbour gets a touch ahead of schedule, and starts letting off the gun an instant before one has missed the bird. After watching me for a while, some neighbours conclude that this policy is fair enough, since precedent makes it unlikely that anything I address will come down. Dear me, as I write, what moments of shame and guilt course through the mind's eye. I am not sure any of us can claim a pure record of unselfishness, if we have suffered a morning of frustration, not getting much to shoot at, while our neighbours blazed away.

One day not long ago, I was in the middle of the line at a high bird shoot where at one drive the birds turned aside in clouds, forty yards in front of my peg. Everything veered either left or right. I did my best to cut off some of the leftward ones, to discover when I took off my ear defenders that a neighbour had been bawling at me in outrage throughout the drive. I was honestly uncertain whether she had a point or not, but was consoled by the reflection that it was pretty rich for one of the rudest women in Britain to offer instruction in shooting manners.

Unsporting behaviour becomes interesting only when

it is original. One of the best poaching stories – the other sort – which I have heard came from Hugh Millais, son of Raoul the sporting artist and a deadly shot on his day, as well as the finest raconteur north of the Watford Gap. Hugh described how, years ago, he was invited stalking by the rough but matey brother of a Scots girlfriend of the moment. This bloke, who professed himself passionately committed to the pursuit of deer – 'It's ma life' – drove Hugh miles out into the wilderness, and walked him a good many miles more, before they found and felled a large stag. Only as they dragged away the corpse did Hugh perceive something familiar about the landscape. He realised that they were stalking the forest of his own brother. His host was a proud professional poacher who spent his days covertly removing beasts from every estate within a hundred miles. Hugh's story is that he was a hapless pawn in this man's hands. Those who know Millais have their own ideas.

I came across an eighteenth-century painting recently of a Landgrave of Hesse-Darmstadt shooting pheasants. The scene is set in darkness, pierced by a huge lantern held by a lackey. The Landgrave is aiming at a roost-Ing pheasant situated, at a generous estimate, ten yards from his muzzle. Presumably he was proud of what he was doing or he would not have encouraged a court painter to immortalise the scene. Likewise, Colonel Peter

Hawker, high priest of early-nineteenth-century sportsmen, loved to crawl up on flocks of unsuspecting geese
and assault them with an enormous fowling piece. When
it came to partridge-shooting, Hawker described how he
cantered in pursuit of coveys until they dropped, fired
when they rose again, took up the chase, and so on until
the last exhausted birds fell victim to his prowess. It doesn't
sound much like sport, but *autre temps* and all that.

The Victorians liked deer drives, where the beasts were
herded past to be shot by relays of rifles. Admiral Beatty,
he of the First World War battle-cruisers, in his retirement enjoyed crawling around with a shotgun, stalking
grouse coveys and potting them on the ground. It seems
an odd pastime, but it made him happy. In the same
way, few of us nowadays want to spend our Saturday
afternoons cheering on lions as they dismember flushes of
Christians, but some Premier League Roman sportsmen
found this more pleasing than watching Man U. I have a
nasty feeling that gladiatorial combat would find a ready
modern audience if it was revived in the Colosseum every
Saturday afternoon.

My point is that each successive generation makes its
own value judgements about what is or is not sporting. If
we shudder at pole traps and think that things our ancestors did were a bit off, so they would look askance at
some of our antics. What, for instance, would they make
of stalkers who insist on being carried by Argocat to
within a quarter-mile of the shot? My own conscience in
this department was tested recently on a hill in Angus.
The stalker and I walked vainly all morning in hot sunshine, four or five miles of stiff going. By lunchtime I was

exhausted. Late in the afternoon we spied stags from the Land Rover. The stalker said, 'We'll cheat a bit here.' He took the vehicle far round and over the summit behind the deer. We then had less than a mile to walk down on to them. The beast which I shot walked on four hundred yards before it dropped. Karen Blixen wrote of a Swedish friend who was christened by his Kenyan gun-bearers *'Resase Modja'* – 'One Cartridge'. Here is a title every hunter aspires to. That day in Angus, I came home feeling less than a proper sportsman on two counts: we had not really done the walking, and I had not killed the stag cleanly.

With stalking and vehicles, there is no simple right or wrong answer, save that most of us want to feel we have worked for our beasts. Likewise, it is hard to take a definitive line about how far it is sporting to push birds. On a lot of shoots, and especially grouse moors, one cover is filled from the last. It makes many of us queasy, however, to see partridges at some commercial shoots driven to and fro across the same valley all morning. I am increasingly uncomfortable about the practice of leaving the pick-up until the end of the drive. If the objective is to cause our quarry a minimum of suffering, it seems right to send a dog after a runner as soon as it falls. First, this much increases the chance of finding the bird. Second, it can be killed more quickly – perhaps twenty or thirty minutes sooner, in a long drive. Likewise, it often seems unsporting to take a shot at a very high bird which one is unlikely to kill. The odds are that it will fly on carrying several pellets.

Low birds pose different problems. I am interested by

the attitude of some serious big shots I know. While we middle-class types agonise about whether to shoot, professional killers mow down low birds without blinking. Their radar engages any flying object, super-high, high, middling, low, deck-level, and drops it by reflex before the brain engages. I suspect the same ruthlessness, allied to consummate skill, is what made the 'Red Baron' von Richthofen an ace of the air back in 1916.

Fly fishing lends itself less readily to unsporting practices, if one excludes super-Flashman tactics such as stroke-hauling and dynamiting pools. Most fishermen have growing doubts about whether it is fair any longer to kill large numbers of salmon, even when the opportunity is there. Personally, after taking three or four for the freezer, if we are lucky enough to get so many, I feel no regret about releasing those that follow. I blush to remember the days when we killed everything. The great Hugh Falkus gave dire warnings about the perils of catch-and-release. He said this undermined the very basis of the justification for game fishing – that we eat our quarry. Yet Falkus was a man of his generation. Today, few of us believe that the future of angling will be determined by ironclad adherence to the principle of slaying what we catch. It seems out of kilter with the spirit of the times to kill salmon in dozens on a single beat in a single week.

There now, what have I forgotten? Of course. No essay of this kind can convincingly be completed without consulting the oracle, the supreme authority on caddish sporting behaviour, the 'minor sprig of the Shires aristocracy' who writes begging letters inviting himself to shoot. Damn. I've lost his number.

13
Naver Magic

'CONDITIONS ARE PERFECT,' said David the gillie. I responded: 'I've been waiting for thirty years to hear a gillie say that.' You know how any river usually is: too low or too high, too coloured or too bright. Fishermen acquire grey hairs listening to tales of the forty salmon taken last week, of the thirty certain for next, while circumstances right now – which happens to be when oneself is casting a fly – are deemed hopeless. Yet here we were on the Naver, prettiest salmon river in Scotland, on a late June day when colour was going out of the water, the level was falling steadily, and only showers were forecast. I fished the Naver for years a decade or two ago, and learned to love it as I have loved no other Highland river for the variety of the beats, heathery upper streams and leafy lower stretches. I abandoned the river as a tenant after suffering arid, barren, expensive summer weeks three years running. I was now back in bliss as a guest.

That first sunny morning, I hooked a grilse which tore around the pool for five minutes before slipping off just as David put out the net. I reminded myself of the soft mouths of grilse, and regretted applying side strain as the fish hung in mid-current. A few minutes later, I hooked another which was on and off within seconds. David urged me to hand line more energetically, to force a strong take. I was taught to work a fly slowly, but I almost always accept a gillie's advice. I stripped line hard, and was rewarded ten minutes later with a five-pound grilse on the bank. My wife, who had begun to think herself a jinxed fisher, was euphoric when she landed two that morning. Ever since she caught her first fish on the Naver ten years ago, the river can do no wrong in her eyes.

I worked hard all afternoon on Beat One, at the top of the river, and around teatime caught another grilse in the Dal Mallart pool. Then, when the gillies went home, I started at the top of the beat again. Much as I enjoy company, there is a charm about fishing alone which never fades. Successes and failures are all one's own. I cast painstakingly down the Crack and Dal Mallart, Brown's and Dal Harrald. Around 7 p.m., I waded across the river to fish the long, wide bay at the tail of Dal Mallart from the far bank. Few fish had been showing on the surface, but suddenly they began to throw themselves about, a sight which makes most of us redouble our efforts. At the very bottom of the pool, in flat water just beside a rock, there was a swirl around my Willie Gunn. The fish bent the rod thrillingly for ten minutes before I netted him.

Early next morning, full of eagerness, I was wading the Syre pool, a place of happy memories from twenty years ago, and for many Naver fishers the most fascinating rendezvous on the river. For the past fortnight, the gillies said, Syre had been blank. Beat Two seemed out of favour with salmon. Anyway, I was there and I loved the pool, and was determined to test it. A consequence of getting a bit older is that one is less keen on rough wading. Being absurdly tall, even sober I possess the balance of a drunken Leinsterman. I hate big stones on the bottom and I hate falling in. I was moving cautiously, thanking heaven for a strong downstream breeze. About halfway down, a fish pulled the fly hard, which made me concentrate. There is a place at the bottom where an eddy on the far bank curls around a rock. Every regular Naver fisher gets lucky there sometime. I was just starting to think about breakfast as my fly drifted past that rock. I stopped doing so when there was a fierce, strong take.

I had barely clambered onto the bank, reeling fast, when the fish threw itself out of the water, revealing a serious salmon. Now, although I had caught some good fish on Tweed, it was a while since I hooked one in the north of Scotland. I was determined to land it, which meant being more patient and careful than wives and gillies say I usually am. For fifteen minutes that fish bored hither and thither across the pool, refusing to show itself again, but giving me a long view of my backing, and making me nervous about the clumsy knot with which I had connected it to the line. Shaking with excitement, I reflected that one's heart really does bang like a bass drum at these moments, or at least mine is prone to.

I refused to push my luck by getting the net out until the fine spade tail showed. When I did so, haste nearly undid me. It took four or five thrusts before that fish was flopping on the bank. The hook slipped out of its jaws before I could touch it, but there were thirteen pounds of glittering beauty. I told my wife that I didn't care what happened for the rest of the day. I was content. Any serious Russia or Iceland fisher is curling his lip by now, and saying: So what? Yet the thrill of catching a salmon in Scotland never palls for some of us. No experience abroad can match it. More important, it was a joy to glimpse the Naver, once among the great salmon rivers of Scotland, show a glimpse of its old form, after being given a chance by the weather.

I caught two more fish and my wife had three before we took the plane home after a mere two and a half days in the stream. I was in anguish about having to quit in the midst of a banquet, but work sometimes maddeningly interrupts the things which really matter in life. I hope that the river's return to glory goes on and on. The owners deserve it, after some sadly lean years. And so too does that peerless stretch of water, which God intended to be bursting with salmon.

14

With the Beaters

ONE OF THE conceits that sometimes overtakes shooters is to think of the sport simply in terms of the eight or nine people who fire their guns at a driven day. Yet, in reality, every outing embraces some twenty or thirty other people for whom the occasion means at least as much as it does to the guns, even if they are getting paid a little money for their contributions. I am thinking, of course, of the beaters and pickers-up. In most places, guns vary from week to week. It is the home team that provides the continuity, the sense of community, which is indispensable to a happy shoot. Many beaters have been tapping out the same woods and game crops for ten, fifteen, twenty seasons. They know every whim of October partridges and December pheasants at Long Copse or Ten Acre. If guns don't notice each other's performance at a big drive, beaters always do.

A few months ago I begged a place in the beating line at our local shoot, and abandoned my tweed cap and Schoffel in favour of leggings, a camouflaged windproof last worn on East Falkland twenty-something years ago,

and a Carter's Countrywear baseball cap. Saturday at
10 a.m. found me flagging my way along a wooded hillside amid a dozen like-minded spirits, with Peter the
keeper shouting imprecations at us to keep a line, hold
up on the left, take it nice and slow, and all the other
things keepers have been shouting at beaters since time
immemorial. Several times when he called out to me, I
deluded myself that he was saying: 'Put that dog in!' In
truth, of course, he wanted me to 'Get that dog in!' I
broke it to him that I am hopelessly deaf, obeyed orders,
and after that we got on fine. 'Nobody does it for the
money, do they?' said a carpenter named Geoff. 'It's the
day out.' And so, of course, it is. The core members of
that beating team, of whom the oldest was seventy-
two, have been meeting for years at the same shoot every
Saturday, and a few other days as well.

Peter the keeper is a handsome man who wears his
natural authority lightly. This was his nineteenth season.
If you saw him in the street, you would sense at once that
he is in charge of something, even if you were not sure
what. He runs fifty days a year for three shoots embracing
six thousand acres. The young, he said, don't seem to care
for beating any more. The three boys in the line with us
had turned up simply for the money. Among the older
men, some have no interest in shooting themselves, even
when given the chance on beaters' days. It is the fellowship
of sharing an outing in the countryside that brings them
together, rain or shine.

Birds began to burst from the brambles and break
noisily forward through the trees. I felt a sense of personal
failure whenever a pheasant turned back over my head,

or slipped low out of the side of the cover. Either I was letting the side down, or the birds were growing crafty. Stanley, my lab, took a while to learn the rules of this new game. At every drive he found a wounded bird or two as we worked our way forward, but he was slow to get the hang of flushing them, because nobody had ever asked him to do it before. I experimented with making 'brrr, brrr' noises as we marched, without generating much action from the birds, and eventually settled for 'Aye–aye–aye–*aye*!'

A barrage of gunfire echoed across the hillside towards us. In one sense, beating is an odd business, because it can seem so remote from the fevered activity of the guns when they are out of sight. We halted as each flush broke forward, then flapped the flags as silence descended again. It was a dull, still, dry day. David, a burly veteran who was deputy chieftain of the beating line, shouted with impeccable courtesy: 'Please slow it down on the right! Please come round a bit this way!' I demanded: would he say 'please' if I weren't there? 'Oh yes,' said somebody. 'He's just naturally polite.' 'Bet you wish you'd never got off your tractor, Thomas,' cried someone to a beater who was feeling the weight of the walk, and lagging behind us a little.

The horn sounded. We broke forth into a field at the end of the cover, watching guns a hundred yards away gathering birds and gossiping. 'They average about three cartridges for one through the season,' said Peter. A beater remarked that not a lot had come down. Somebody else said it didn't matter. The sceptical voice said: 'Well, there's not a lot of point in all this unless they hit a few.' The line was only teasing, however. The mood was over-whelmingly good-natured, happy, companionable.

At lunch in the pub, a little knot of veterans gathered at their usual private table, while the rest of us spread ourselves around the bar. The guns had their own lunch in the next room. Beaters on this estate receive £17, together with sausages, chips and a pint. The shoot captain says he thinks this is better than giving them £20 and leaving them to eat sandwiches in a cold farmyard. How right he is. An enthusiastic woman beater fell into conversation with Geoff the carpenter. They were talking with unbridled passion about food: 'Don't you think Nigella's lamb in pomegranate sauce is the most wonderful thing you've ever tasted?' I eavesdropped disbelievingly. Yes, they were serious foodies, connoisseurs of the art of Jamie Oliver, Gary Rhodes and the divine Nigella. 'And don't think it's just us,' said Geoff, gesturing to the veteran beaters' table. 'They're all just as keen. One of them gave me a recipe for parsnips the other day: parboil, cover in parmesan and roast – it was wonderful!' We know the jokes about how beaters' cars are usually smarter than those of guns these days, but somehow I never expected to find a beating line getting heavy about Nigella Lawson.

Back on the trailer after lunch, everybody settled into his accustomed place on the bales, the young boys puffing furiously at their Player's as young boys do. We trundled across a few miles of west Berkshire to the last drive. We blanked-in a big wood for twenty minutes, emerging just as a convoy of 4 × 4s arrived, bringing the guns back from lunch. Nice life for some, I thought. If it had been pouring with rain, I could imagine myself getting quite chippy about other people's cushy sporting lives.

I am never quite sure whether birds that fly from one spinney to another during blanking-in are ever persuaded to flush energetically again fifteen minutes later. But it is all part of the game. We trudged uphill for a few hundred yards to the start of the drive. 'We could do with thirty beaters here,' said Peter the keeper, contemplating six acres of thickly brambled woodland. We plunged forward. There were a lot of birds in that cover, and I doubt that we got more than half of them into the air. They soared above the trees, heading for the guns at an altitude that risked upsetting the Heathrow flight path.

I had been lucky enough to visit a really terrible shoot earlier in the season, where the keeper had no idea how to drive a wood or place a line of guns. That experience helped me to perceive how well this lot were doing today. They didn't even look as tired as I felt after all that blanking-in. 'We're always rude about the shooting,' said Geoff wryly, 'and then we get to beaters' day, and we don't do any better than they do.' There was a roar of ironic applause from the beaters when it was announced, after the drive, that 121 shots had been fired to pick up twenty-two pheasants. I looked around the grinning faces. They'll all be there next season. They are much more a part of the fabric of the countryside than most guns. Without their enthusiasm, driven shooting could not exist.

15

Every Shot a Record

$\mathcal{M}$Y FATHER ASSERTED that gamebooks are personal conceits, to be treated with scepticism, if not disbelief. Yet they possess a fascination for sportsmen, and most of us love to leaf through examples when they are open to access. A remarkable example sits beside the billiard table in a Yorkshire shooting lodge and deserves a wider readership. It is the personal record of a Victorian who signed himself simply J. Lamont. It details his shooting experiences between 1886 and 1899. He was tenant, at various periods, of Gunnerside, Reeth and Barningham in Yorkshire and Culford in Suffolk, and owned the six-thousand-acre Knockdow estate in Argyll. Sport was his obsession, and in those days that did not mean Premier League football.

You have never heard of J. Lamont? Nor had I. Yet if his gamebook is to be believed, he was a 'big shot' in the same league as Lords Ripon and Walsingham. His first page notes, on 1 February 1886, in triumphant capital letters: 'The past has been THE VERY BEST SEASON'S SPORT I ever had in my life. I SHALL NEVER LIVE

TO SEE SUCH ANOTHER!' He reports that he killed on the Blackwater in Ireland 214 spring salmon in fifty-seven days, averaging twelve pounds. On his best day, he caught twelve fish totalling 170 pounds.

The story gets more remarkable. Lamont writes that in the same season, he shot 2,063 driven grouse to his own gun in thirty-three days' shooting, with 3,883 cartridges. On his best day he killed 218 grouse with 340 cartridges. He also records 6,810 head of other game at Culford, for 11,214 cartridges. His total for the season was therefore 8,873 head for 15,097 cartridges, in 122 days. His average was 59 per cent. He computed an average of 72.7 birds a day, for 123.74 cartridges. His annual average thereafter attained peaks of 60 per cent in 1887 and 1891, until there was a terrible falling-off to 54 per cent in the late 1890s, when presumably he gave up shooting in disgust.

It proved easy to identify the author by a little research in *Who was Who*. He was Sir James Lamont, chief of Clan Lamont, born in 1828, and thus around sixty at the time of his greatest sporting triumphs. Educated at Rugby, he spent two years in the army and thereafter travelled extensively in Africa and the Arctic. He wrote two books about his experience: *Seasons with the Seahorses* and *Yachting in the Arctic Seas*. He married a daughter of Sir George Denys, with whom he had three children, one, curiously enough, named Norman. He contested three elections unsuccessfully before serving three years as Liberal MP for Bute in the 1860s, and was given a baronetcy in 1910. He owned a house in Mayfair, though he cannot have seen much of it. That mine of historical information *The Highland Sportsman and Tourist* for 1886 eulogises

Knockdow's splendours, and notes that there is an excellent yacht anchorage nearby. Lamont was also a member of the Turf Club.

He must have been a nightmare to shoot with, never mind to live with. Any man capable of recording his own scores with such fanatical care presumably never raised a gun to a bird unless there was a better than 50 per cent chance of killing the poor doomed creature. One can imagine the emotional scenes behind his peg or butt after a drive, if anyone picked a bird which he believed his own. We must assume that he really did kill something like these prodigious quantities of game, and that he was indeed a remarkable shot. This was an era when individual scores of grouse were listed against each gun's name, heaping ignominy upon those who could not keep up with the Lamonts. There are grim days when he notes in red ink: 'Very bad shooting!' He was not, of course, referring here to his own performance.

Doctors and parsons were occasionally invited to join the Lamont party, and must often have wished they had not been. On 6 September 1886, for instance, while the laird credited himself with ninety grouse, a hapless Dr Livesay hit only twenty-six. Colonel Mildmay Wilson was in cracking form through his stay, and one day shot seventy-two grouse while Sir F. Denys – presumably Lamont's brother-in-law – killed a mere twenty-two. The author recorded even the fact that he sold 2,553 head of dead grouse from his moors that season for a total of £298, an average price of two shillings and fourpence apiece, let us say about £9 in modern purchasing power. Grouse were much costlier in those days than in our own.

In 1893 the author was rash enough to let some shooting, which was not at all helpful to estate bags. He noted crossly: 'Mr Phillips and party VB shots!' When grouse were wild, the Lamonts resorted to kites to keep them sitting tight, a common Victorian technique. When nothing else was available to kill, the frustrated laird turned to rabbits. He and a relation killed 330 around his park in August 1887. That year, he shot 111 days, thirty-one of these in Yorkshire; thirteen thousand rabbits were warrened on his ground.

There were occasional brief pauses in the slaughter, when Lamont recorded visits to London, presumably to purchase new instruments of death and consult specialists about deafness. No man who shot as he did, in an age when ear defenders were unknown, could have heard a word anyone said beyond middle age.

There were seldom more than four or five guns in his parties, presumably to ensure that nobody was out of the shooting for more than three minutes. Yet even Lamont suffered moments of doubt about overdoing it. At Culford on 17 December 1886, his team shot 647 head. He wrote in red ink: 'Too many pheasants: 500 enough.' The RSPB would applaud.

Lamont's biggest year was 1885, when he claimed 8,873 head of game for 15,097 cartridges. In the 1890s, his annual bags tapered off steeply, until in 1899 he shot just 416 head, and fired only 775 cartridges. The numbers become wearisome, as no doubt they did to the birds, but Lamont's record makes fascinating reading. It seems odd to most of us, more than a century later, that any man could choose to devote so much time to slaughter on such a scale. Yet that is what Victorian and Edwardian big shots did, earning the plaudits of their contemporaries. I am glad I never met James Lamont, but his gamebook possesses an enduring fascination. He died at the age of eighty-five in 1913. It was an entirely appropriate moment for him to quit his world, a year before it vanished forever.

One day last season I found myself shooting in a line alongside a modern Lamont, one of those men who regularly feature in lists of the fifty – or even fewer – best shots in the country. This happens from time to time. I assume that it reflects a conspiracy by hosts to seed the draw, and put me in my place as a sportsman. I am not sure whether they also intend the consequence, which is to make me contemplate giving up shooting altogether. Ace marksmen make the whole thing seem so maddeningly easy. They pick off long crossing birds and high overhead ones, snap shots on the flank and the odd one so far behind that it is in danger of getting mixed up with the next drive. Although we try not to be mean-spirited about these things, it becomes tempting to cheer whenever some hapless creature escapes the laser eye of a supershot.

If one has not met a given star before, he can often be identified by a glance in the back of his vehicle. It is fitted with customised compartments and drawers to house every known shooting gadget, as well as dogs prematurely aged by the exertion of gathering master's bag eighty or ninety days a year. On grouse moors, at each drive the serious shot's first act is to set a marker card on the front of the butt. I thought of buying one of these charming little accessories last year, but finally resisted. I am not superstitious, but it would have been a temptation to providence. I convinced myself that once I owned a marker, nobody would ever again invite me to shoot grouse. And even if they did, I would never hit enough to need to chalk the casualties on a card. In my case, anyway, most of what comes down is still fit to run a marathon between hitting the heather and being picked out of it, and thus its point of landing bears scant relationship to its likely pick-up place.

Superstars never run out of cartridges, partly because they are ammunitioned for a siege, and partly because they do not waste many. They usually fire fewer shots than you or me, because the second barrel is redundant unless there is a right-and-left on offer. My own performance deteriorates sharply when neighbours are conducting a chainsaw massacre. Instead of concentrating coolly on what I am supposed to be doing, I start fantasising about the cartoon bubble hanging above the next-door butt, whose occupant is saying to himself: 'Why do they waste useful birds on chaps who can't hit a barn door?'

Some supershots, however, are also generous ones. I stood next to James Percy on a day when every grouse seemed to be making a foolish career decision to head for him rather than me. Noticing this, he left several that he could well have killed before they reached me. I was suitably grateful. Some other aces, by contrast, are greedy shots as well as deadly ones. One becomes a bit fed up when a pile of birds gathers in front of one's peg, killed by the neighbouring deadeye two seconds before one pulls a trigger. He is right, of course, in supposing that left to me, those birds would have survived to draw pensions. But it hurts to have the message rubbed in. At the end of each drive at the aforementioned shoot last season, as we picked up my neighbour bustled over and demanded: 'Have you got any extras?' By this, of course, he meant: 'I suspect that your dog has collected several birds which properly belong to me.' Since the aforesaid corpses lay around my butt, he was undoubtedly right. I denied all knowledge.

That day, the only target I could have hit with assurance was my neighbour. His view of the exercise echoed that of W. G. Grace, to his opponent at an exhibition match: 'These people have come to see me bat, not you bowl.' The experience provided a flavour of what it must have been like to shoot with Victorian big shots like James Lamont, who obsessively counted and recorded cartridges and kills, measuring their own performances as if they were establishing an Olympic record, as indeed they often were.

A supershot reading the whinges above might respond something like this: 'Writing is your business, and you take it very seriously. Shooting is mine. If you were as good as I am, you might see it the same way. Without one or two people like me in a line, especially on a grouse moor, the bag would be half what it should be. Surely all of us go shooting to do the same thing – kill some birds. I just happen to be better at it than you are.' All this is perfectly true. We need the absolutely dedicated, single-minded shots as much as we need a first team in any other sport. There is a strand of crude envy in my own remarks. Yet some very good shots manage to go about their business in a wonderfully relaxed and good-natured fashion. At any shoot with any team of guns, there is uncertainty about who shot certain birds. As to picking-up, I get furious if the professionals' dogs grab everything before my beast has had a go, but it becomes pedantic to worry about which gun or which dog has gathered every single bird.

For most of us, shooting is a pastime. What matters is to savour the countryside in good company. This attitude is probably corrosive to success, but I don't mind. I simply want to enjoy the party and the beauty of the experience, and if possible have a few laughs. Nothing is more depressing than those mercifully rare shoots where the atmosphere resembles that of a state funeral, even before it starts raining or the team sits down to a rotten lunch. Just as weekend tennis players are likely to enjoy ourselves more if we play with each other, rather than venture on court with Wimbledon finalists, so it tends to be most fun to shoot among people of roughly one's own standard, if that many bunglers can be found. When I hear other guns chattering earnestly about variable chokes and a new fast cartridge, I know that I have come to the wrong place. I am happy to leave the fanatics to play with each other, and would rather not find any latter-day J. Lamont next to me.

16

An Idyll in Kenya

Each morning began with the chiding chuckle of Henry the hornbill, as we christened him, high in a yellow fever tree beside our room shortly after six. Soon afterwards, Henry fluttered down to perch on the window frame, from whence he hammered fiercely on the glass. He did not tap. Instead, addressing his own reflection, that bird's big, ugly beak banged so hard that we expected him to break through at any second, and shooed him away. The sharp, glittering early light is one of the greatest beauties of Africa, a revelation each time the sun rises beyond the hills. After a quick lap of the swimming pool amid mist rising from its deliciously chilly water, we pulled on jeans and boots and walked down to the stables — no more than a framework of rough timber supporting a sunshade of corrugated iron. We led out the horses among the ducks bickering in the dust underfoot, and set off for two hours in the saddle which were among the most precious joys of the day.

The view of the bush seemed to stretch for an eternity. We were gazing perhaps thirty miles towards the low blue mountains on the horizon. As we breasted the hill that led up to the dirt airstrip, zebra stirred, trotting idly to put a few yards between themselves and us. There were clusters of gazelle and oryx, the odd ostrich strutting pompously, a waterbuck, a few heavy eland. Gazing from end to end of our vision amid the dusty yellow grass riffling in the breeze, we reckoned we could see at least five hundred, perhaps nearer a thousand, head of African plains game kicking dust within a mile of our horses, their delicate shades seemingly floodlit by the early sun, or silhouetted on the horizon. On and on through them we rode as the sun began to lift. 'Snake,' said Mutegi the syce monosyllabically, abruptly jerking his reins sideways, and gesturing us to do likewise. Most ranches pay a bounty for puff-adders, which kill a lot of sheep because the poor woollies are too stupid to be frightened of them.

Syce is the Indian word for a groom. Like so much else to do with empire, it travelled a century ago from the subcontinent to Kenya, and has stayed there. Mutegi saw everything maybe twenty seconds before we did: snakes, impala, giraffe, elephants. How can one miss a dozen elephants? Amazingly easily, until after seeing them out there week after week our eyes too began to adjust to the muted shades in which the bush hides even its outsize fauna from intruders.

And so home, to breakfast in heaven. I have loved Africa, and especially Kenya, for years. I have always nursed a dream of not merely holidaying there, but living the bush life for a while. Because I am a writer, and writers can write anywhere, a day came when there seemed nothing to stop us fleeing from the rains and frosts of English February to pass five weeks in a farmhouse we rented amidst the Kamogi cattle ranch high on the Laikipia Plateau, five hours by road from Nairobi, and an eternity from the troubles of mankind.

The homestead is a cluster of thatched stone buildings set around a garden laid out to borders of exotic plants and shrubs, looking out upon a reed-fringed lake, with only the bush beyond. It was built by a Northern Irish army officer who bought the ranch on a whim half a century ago, and whose family have lived there ever since. We fell in love with it at first sight. It is a perfect example of the British genius for creating an island of Britishness in the heart of Africa, full of the incongruous bric-a-brac of a family home. There are elephant bones on the dining table and polo sticks in the sitting room, school photographs everywhere, forgotten novels and aged London glossy magazines and crates of vodka and a grand piano and dogs and old tennis rackets and – well, what more do you want to feel at home in Africa, for heaven's sake? Country life in Kenya today is pretty much what it must have been like in England a century ago – not for the Hastings ancestors, I hasten to add, who were living in places like Camberwell at that period, but for the people who were bossing us about.

In Kenya one never has to waste time saying 'What a perfect day,' because every day in February, and most of the rest of the year, is perfect. We settled into a routine that remained unbroken day after day: swim, ride, eat, work, eat, sleep, work, drive out to find animals, play tennis, drink before the blazing wood fire, eat, sleep. After a few weeks of this, we were healthier and fitter than we have been for years. Penny, my wife, has decided that sleeping under a mosquito net is cosy. She is demanding one at home. Ordering groceries from the delightfully named Settlers' Stores in Nanyuki, a mere two hours down what we might laughingly call the road, has a charm quite absent from a trip to Tesco.

By a quirk of technology, a satellite beam runs across the ranch, a couple of miles from the house. After bumping up a ragged, rutted track towards a low hill where stands a solitary Samburu tribesman's hut, encircled by a *boma* of thorns to protect the family goats, it is possible to get a connection on an English mobile telephone. Once a week, feeling slightly mad, we stood in the wilderness solemnly clutching our phones, contemplating a distant bustard and being contemplated by a couple of bemused tribesmen leaning on their spears, as we made sure that our children were in one piece. A friend produced the worst line in Africa during one of these communions with the outside world. A herd of game trotted down the road. When a London voice answered his call, he said: 'Hello,

darling. I'm at a zebra crossing.' We groaned and sent
him to Coventry.

Beyond the child checks, we basked in ignorance. We
saw no newspapers. We heard no radio. We watched no
television. And it was wonderful. A friend teased me
before we left London: 'Tony Blair will have resigned
by the time you get back, and you'll have missed it all.'
Sucks. After the first few days, we thought nothing of
the world outside. We cared only about whether the elephants would come down to the lake to drink that
evening; whether Mungai, our sublime cook, had caught
enough crayfish at the dam for one of his home-made
pasta and crayfish feasts; how the weavers were getting
along with building a nest in the tree a few feet from our
breakfast table. We were cushioned from every normal
modern care. If we want to do something at home – hold
a dinner party, arrange a picnic, go for a ride, skim the
pool – there is nobody but ourselves to do the business.
At Kamogi, it was bliss merely to express a desire and have
it fulfilled by others, who also sorted out the wreckage
afterwards.

Sometimes of a morning, as I sat at my laptop in the
little office writing a book, Richard, the tall, loose-limbed
young Turkana farm manager, put his head in. 'We're
castrating cattle up by the airstrip,' he would say. 'Would
anyone like to come?' Or it might be: 'We're going to kill
a sheep for the house.' 'There are giraffe by the dam.'
'We're going to dip the stock.' And all these things seemed
more important and interesting than anything that might
be happening four thousand miles away, at home.
Richard, who has an encyclopaedic knowledge of local

wildlife, was charmingly eager to involve us in the daily business of the ranch. Forty-five men, just five of them English-speaking, work on its ten thousand acres, living with their families in a cluster of round thatched huts, each one perhaps twelve feet in diameter, that stand a hundred yards beyond the garden. Sometimes we chafed a little at the language barrier, if only because we wanted to identify a bird or wildflower. But somehow we understood enough of each other to convey some rough meaning in monosyllables without Swahili.

Kenya possesses the widest range of bird species in Africa, and most seemed to breakfast in the garden. We came to know them all: the brilliant red sunbird; the firefinch with its delicate shading; the exquisitely-named cordon bleu, with pale blue breast. Much as I love the English countryside, at home I have never been a serious birdwatcher because I have always told myself I do not have the time. Yet once one settled into a pace deliciously slower than that of west Berkshire, suddenly there seemed to be hours in which to notice all manner of wonders. In Africa, the wilderness is always pressing upon you. Early one morning, when elephants appeared behind the stables, I was intrigued that even old Kanobia the gardener, who has seen more of the great beasts than I have had hot dinners, dashed down to see them, excited as the rest of us. Their majesty remains irresistible, even after a thousand sightings. It seemed specially wonderful to glimpse them as a natural part of the landscape, rather than in a game park or – far worse – a zoo.

The bush crowded up to the very edge of the tennis court for the last set in the evening light. Its animal sounds echoed from the trees as we sat with a drink under the stars outside the dining room. A frog hopped casually into the room in which I wrote, while lizards watched my labours curiously from high on the wall above. One of our guests saw a huge tortoise shell outside her hut. Peering curiously, she started back in surprise when a rather cross tortoise head appeared from under the carapace, made unfriendly noises, then laboured heavily away across the grass. One night we had a difference of opinion with a speckled pigeon, about whether animal rights included roosting space in our bedroom. After a sharp tussle and a lot of angry fluttering, the pigeon lost the argument and was expelled. I told friends who came to stay that they were forbidden to bring newspapers, and in consequence there was an unkind and unsuccessful conspiracy to persuade me that the government had fallen.

For the first few days I sometimes fancied that I heard a telephone ring, then perceived that it was a mere insect or froggy noise. The only sounds that broke that the huge silence, save those of nature, came from the small plane which fetched and carried our guests. I greeted each new contingent by saying, 'Welcome to paradise,' and meant it. All manner of problems, of the kind which cause infinite vexation at home, receded into proper insignificance. When one of the rickety old 4 × 4s broke down in the bush on a night drive and it took two hours for Buni the driver to fetch some help and get home, what it did matter? Nobody wants modern cars with lots of electronics out here. Instead, transport depends on vintage Land Rovers whose ailments can be addressed with a kick and a pair of pliers, as ours frequently were. If the taps ran dry for a few hours, who cared?

About now, some readers will mutter: 'It's all right for *him*, being able to swan off for five weeks. But what about real people with real lives in England?' Yes and no. True, I am a writer who can work anywhere, with grown-up children. But Kenya today offers wonderful things for everybody, and it is not essential to be either a lotus-eater or a millionaire to rent a house there. The world's neurotics, some of them in the Foreign Office and the US State Department, have convinced themselves that it is a venue where one is likely to be blown up by the local Al Q'aeda cell. In the bit of Kenya we go to, one is more likely to die of contentment.

Staying in one place abroad, doing one's own thing with one's own friends, has much to recommend it over staying in hotels. True, in a park like the Mara or Serengeti one is almost guaranteed a sight of all the great animals, whereas only one party among our lot has glimpsed lion while out riding, and we have never seen leopard. But it seems so much more pleasing to bump into game wherever it chances to be, here or there around a working ranch, rather than to inspect it in an enclosure where one shares every sighting with six minibuses of chattering Japanese.

One morning when we had ridden out to a lake for a bush breakfast, while we were eating and watching the pelicans Richard reported with a laconic giggle: 'Horses run off.' Our mounts had seized the opportunity presented by a day-dreaming minder to canter home to their stable. In England, I would have been livid. Under the fleecy clouds and blue sky of Kamogi, we simply joined Richard in laughter. In ordinary modern life, time is the commodity out of which most of us cheat ourselves. In Africa, there always seem to be luxurious picnic hampers full of time. 'I feel as if we were living out *White Mischief* without the mischief,' said my wife one morning. I was left to wonder if she was lamenting the absence of the last bit. In the tiny, bookless primary school hut in the farm village, two thoughts for the day were chalked neatly on the blackboard: 'Jesus is my friend', and 'God created heaven and earth and everything in it in six days'. Your average modern churchman in Britain would find either proposition ridiculous, but deep in the bush both seemed very moving.

In the midst of the day, everything in Africa slows or stops, unless it is air-conditioned. Even the great animals take refuge from the sun, though at six thousand feet on the Laikipia Plateau the heat is always dry and never unbearable. I write until lunch beckons, then join the others lazing by the pool. At teatime, the farm awakes once more. Charming old Kanobia, who has tended the garden for forty years, reappears to water the shrubs. An encouraging clinking of pots and pans begins in the kitchen. We go our separate ways towards tennis court or stables. Penny and I set out on the horses again, grateful for the breeze which keeps off the flies, savouring the creak of saddle leather and clink of bits, watching among the giant euphorbia shrubs the irresistible slow-motion progress of a herd of giraffe. An unkind companion suggested that if I dismounted and joined them, they would welcome me as one of their own. That is the sort of rotten joke people make when one stands six foot six.

Weaving among the bushes, I twisted in the saddle to avoid the thorns which gash an instant's carelessness in a sleeveless shirt, and to listen to an explanation from Richard the manager, who was out with us, about the medicinal properties of one plant, the use of another for local dyestuff. A stunningly handsome young Samburu tribesman, clad only in a brilliant red cotton kilt and several pounds' weight of beads, with ochre-dyed hair and a spear, paused in the midst of the emptiness to chat to Richard. Our respect for this superb figure was slightly diminished when Richard reported that the teenager was looking for a friend's *boma* or family corral, and was lost. Likewise, it seemed incongruous that he should be carrying an electric torch. For heaven's sake, surely only stupid white men from the cities need torches in the bush?

Hector, the ranch's bull terrier, tore off in pursuit of a group of zebra, putting them to flight. One beast kicked out fiercely with his hind legs in retaliation, which served Hector right. We began to pick a path carefully down a long rocky decline, grateful for the horses' surefootedness. The evening light cast a glow upon the hides of the gazelle. A pair of sacred ibis, with those long, slender downturned beaks, flapped gracefully across our path. We turned towards home, past the night guard with his shouldered shotgun and the vegetable garden teeming with all the lush green things that in England belong to July, not February, and even then never grow in such luxuriance.

In the kitchen Mungai the cook, whose skills would impress the brothers Roux, was contriving his nightly masterpiece. How incongruous it seemed, to see on his shelf the works of Jamie Oliver, the River Café and the divine Nigella. Mungai relegates P. G. Wodehouse's Anatole to amateur status. The rations across most of the bits of Africa, I know, are of the school food variety – healthy but dull. By contrast Mungai's soups, soufflés, spinach pancakes, duck with noodles are sensational. Every time I glimpsed the ducks scratching around in the stable yard, I counted them with affectionate interest, like the Walrus among the oysters, to ensure there were enough left to keep inviting them to our noodle feasts until the end of our stay.

After a dinner involving a soufflé and that unfortunate sheep whose fate Richard discussed with me only yesterday, the bridge players got to work in the corner. It seemed droll to reflect that for more than two centuries now, the English have been murmuring 'Two spades,' 'Three diamonds,' to each other in such a setting, a few hundred yards from the nearest elephant. I took down from the shelf *Diseases of Cattle in Tropical Africa*, because that seemed the sort of bedside book one should read at Laikipia, though there were also lots of old novels like *Swallows and Amazons*. Instead of the birds which swooped in and out of the high-ceilinged sitting room during the daylight hours, now in darkness bats replaced them, seeming both friendly and wholly appropriate.

In one sense everything we were doing, the manner in which we lived through those enchanted weeks, represented an illusion: a dream of plenty and tranquillity.

Such a vision is, of course, available only to a handful of exceptionally fortunate people, black and white, in this great continent which is otherwise prey to hardship, poverty, violence and gross misgovernment. No thoughtful person who travels in Africa today, or who lives as we did, can long forget the teeming masses and the perils which are always out there in the vast tracts of lawless cities and bandit-prone bush beyond such tiny islands of bliss as ours, on which a farm worker earns maybe £35 a month and thinks himself lucky to enjoy peace and security. But God, it is such fun – a revelation of what life can offer when, for a season, one allows oneself to forget the relentless kettledrum clamour of the everyday world in which we live, up and down the motorway, in and out of cities, on and off the telephone, bombarded with noise, news, pollution, conflict, the daily diet of what we call civilisation.

My father once had himself cast away alone on a desert island in the Indian Ocean, an experience he richly enjoyed until he contracted scurvy and an impressive range of tropical diseases which caused him to return home on a stretcher. Our own experiment in Africa seems a perfect variation on his. We embrace the solitude and the wilderness, in which we see no vehicle save our own Land Rovers, and scarcely a white face from the outside world. We have all the comforts of home that really matter, even if one is bereft of communications and the putter of the electric generator dies at bedtime.

At last, early on a March morning, Penny and I took a farewell ride. Within a mile of the house we saw giraffe and elephants, eland and zebra, birds innumerable. That afternoon, a little plane circled low over the house, pitched down on the airstrip, whipping up the usual storm of dust, and bore us away, back to our English lives. The first storm of the rainy season was just breaking. We said goodbye to all the ranch people with more sentiment and deeper regret than I have ever known after a mere holiday. Like so many English people, I feel a powerful sense of belonging in Africa. Our forebears were here for so long. Among the people of Kenya, I have seldom met anything but goodwill.

We came home to the usual round of drizzle, terrorist alerts and government bungling. It would be deceitful to pretend that such an escape from reality as ours would work all the time. Those of us who have fed all our lives on a diet of haste, stimulus, tension would wither amid Africa's drowsy timelessness. After five weeks we were ready for a shopping fix, a trip to Covent Garden and even a glimpse of our loved ones. Yet even if we do not seek a permanent escape from the imperfections of our own world, what a privilege it seems, sometimes to gain remission from it.

Kamogi is a rich relic of what life once offered the British across much of Africa – beauty and comfort in the midst of a great wilderness. We have started to count the days until next time. I tell my wife that the situation is quite simple: I never want to go anywhere else again. If one is lucky enough to catch a glimpse of heaven, why go to the other place, or for that matter to the West Indies?

17

Tweed at Autumn

A DULL SUN was showing between the scudding clouds, laying a glitter on the water. The low, grey craft sat apparently motionless in midstream as the boatman pulled steadily against the Tweed current. In the stern, I let incoming line drop in coils to the bottom boards as it slid through my fingers, then lifted the rod for another cast. Some people hate boat-fishing. So indeed did I, once upon a time. But I have grown used to it. After years of visiting the same beat, I have learned to welcome its familiar watermarks: the grassy point off which a fish so often lingers; the ripples above the big rocks; the tangle of flotsam swirling in a backwater below the best pool.

That week, thank heaven, the wind was mostly in abeyance, and when it rose was usually friendly. It is true that no one can call themselves a proper fisher unless they can cope with a breeze. It becomes depressing, however, when the cast hits the water with a curl which means that the fly will not start to ply for five or ten yards. Correspondingly, it is so pleasing when the line shoots out straight, the fly plops cleanly into the current. You know that if a fish is there, it is immediately being shown the lure as temptingly as possible.

People who do not fish often declare that they find the process tedious, the demands on patience too great. Being impatient myself, I am sometimes surprised by how contentedly I can spend hour after hour on the river amid a miscellany of thoughts so trifling that a passing midge might demand more taxing sustenance for its brain. As Peter Wheat has written: 'Each angler will create his personal angling world, in which only he can dwell.' How long has that rippling water taken to flow the long miles from Teviot and from the tiny, distant burns of the Cheviots? How many fishermen's feet does it take in a season to wear those rough, barren patches in the paintwork of the bottom boards beneath me? I watch the leaves and passing fragments of weed racing alongside, and gaze at the trees, somehow more glorious on the banks of Tweed than on any other Scottish river.

In the distance stand two clock towers framed by the roofs and town wall of Coldstream, a classic Border view of the kind that makes me love fishing here, even for slim pickings, rather than in Arctic wastelands where there are far more fish. Coldstream looks wonderfully inviting from a distance, much more so than when standing in its grey high street. Once I asked a boatman the identity of the stone figure who stands atop the great column at the eastern end of the town. He shrugged over the oars. It seemed droll that he should row beneath that statue every day of his life, yet save all his curiosity for the river.

Every fisherman spends many hours peering down upon the unbroken surface of the water, speculating with the intensity of a hopeless love affair about what is passing invisibly beneath. Is a salmon at this moment lying on the bottom, fins flicking rhythmically as it gazes with indifference at the passing fly? Or is the fish aroused, turning, following the fly's path across the current until the moment at which it is whipped from his line of vision, to soar once more through the air at the rod's command? It has taken me years to acknowledge the virtue of allowing the fly to linger in the water, even when the line appears to lie directly behind the boat; to realise that even when the lure seems to have completed its arc, in reality it is still working across the current for a further fifteen or twenty seconds before straightening beneath the rod point. A dog walker pauses to watch from the bank. I am a passionately solitary fisher. I resent spectators even, or perhaps especially, when I am playing a fish. But solitude is a rare luxury in the Borders.

On Tweed I think often of Walter Scott, whose name is inseparably entwined with the river. His novels are little read now, but I adore them. I would recommend Scott's *Journal* to anyone who spends time in his country. It offers a peerless portrait not only of a writer's life, but of how the Borders were 180 years ago. There is a gentle melancholy about the beauty of the region, quite different from the wild joys of the Highlands. Another writer little read today, H. V. Morton, also wrote wonderfully about the Border towns in his travel books of seventy years ago. And beyond these authors, of course, there is always Buchan.

Damn. A loop of line curling beneath the reel has caught the strap of my waders. The cast falls five yards short of where I intended. A Tweed boat is a simple construction, yet I never cease marvelling at how often I manage to catch some protrusion as I throw the line. In a wind, I can conjure a knot out of nothing. 'You'll need to get another couple of yards there,' says the boatman laconically. Yes, yes, I know. As a quick, sharp shower passes, small trout start to rise eagerly beneath both banks. There is a sudden pull at the fly, a few seconds of tension, and then I am impatiently towing a three-pound brownie to the boat side, before flicking him back into the flow. If I were after trout, I would have been seriously excited by that fish. As it is, I am cross with it for offering false promise.

Here, one can see a good quarter-mile downriver, and glimpse the splash of distant salmon if they are there. Not much is showing. By now I should know enough about fishing to recognise that the level of activity on the surface can be quite unrelated to the chances of hooking something. But the sight of a fish jumping within yards of the boat galvanises most of us to try that little bit harder, to give an ounce more concentration to landing the fly gracefully in the stream. A heron flaps clumsily overhead, almost as unlovable as the swans ruffling their feathers as they feed, fifty yards below. How are the other rods doing? I am ashamed to acknowledge that I still suffer from the adolescent disease of always supposing that there is a party next door to which I have not been invited. Here I am, fishing a good beat in wonderful conditions, yet still brooding about what they might be doing on Junction.

The boatman doesn't help, feeding my unworthy

thoughts: 'They got sixteen on Upper Floors yesterday, and one was over thirty pounds.' Whom must I kill, to get to fish Upper Floors? Or, more plausibly, which bank should I rob? The light has changed, as it does almost hourly at this time of year, putting a sheen on the water that makes it hard to see the line. Slowly, the Temple Dog that has served me so well on several rivers this year swings across from the far bank. The line straightens behind the boat. Mindful of the boatman's advice, I leave it lingering for a few seconds more, as I begin to think about tea. Suddenly, the fly pulls. I feel the wonderful power of a salmon. Every pennyworth of my vacuous thoughts escapes into the chilling air, as I focus on a single heavenly reality. He's on.

There seems nothing to beat the first hour of the fishing day. Hopes are at their zenith, undimmed by the disappointment of experience. The boatman rested for a moment on his oars as we bobbed beside the heavy water at the head of the pool and said: 'Right. Off you go, and don't be too quick lifting your fly again. Let it lie a minute behind the boat.' I threw my Comet tube on a short line into the midst of the torrent, watched it whip swiftly round, paused, cast again a yard longer until I was reaching the far eddies. A blustery October breeze sent ripples scurrying across the slack water. Brendan didn't mind. 'When it's as low as this, an east wind can move the fish about almost as much as a spate.' He was rowing briskly now, to check the stern of the boat as it swung with the current.

We all know that fish are as prone to take in slack water as in fast, if there is a lie. But many of us find a special excitement in a pool with a strong flow. I was now fishing the only heavy water on the beat, when the river was relatively low. Fishing in October has the charm of stolen sport, at a season when most anglers have been obliged to put away their rods. On Tweed there is an added thrill of knowing that this is the summit of the river's year, a time when among the big stale brutes which have lingered in fresh water since June or July, there are also plenty of perfect fresh blue-and-silver salmon, some of them monsters. I was concentrating on every movement of the fly, willing the broken waters to reveal a fish. Most hours, most days, most seasons, these imprecations are in vain. It is now a good while since in Scotland I could sustain a boast I was once able to make, of catching an average of a fish for every day with a rod in my hand. On this grey morning, however, I was granted my little miracle. Less than fifteen minutes after we started, the line tightened as it passed the edge of the flow. I lifted the rod, and was into a salmon. 'Did you see his tail?' said Brendan. 'He's a good fish.' I muttered: 'Don't say a word,' and settled over the rod as Brendan beached the boat and stood beside me, net in hand. Like so many Scottish salmon fishers that season, thus far I had enjoyed poor pickings. I desperately wanted to land this fish. Yet as always, within minutes I was in perverse anguish, torn between wanting the thrill of playing it to continue forever, and yearning for the relief of seeing it on the bank.

Like so many big fish, this one did not throw itself about on the surface, but bored into the stream, using the current to hold my rod at bay. I dithered about whether to give it more stick, as many gillies urge, or simply to hold it firm and steady. 'I'm going to take my time, Brendan,' I said. 'I'm damned if I'm going to lose this one.' I conjured the image of the frail hook in the fish, asking myself whether it was merely clinging by a sliver of flesh, or was dug deep into the scissors of its jaws. Apprehensive, I held the rod well bent, while the fish drove away across the current. Ten minutes later Brendan netted it. My heart soared at the sight of its seventeen pounds as much as when I landed the first fish of my life. 'After that, I don't care what happens in the next couple of days,' I said. 'The way Scotland is now, I'm so grateful to have this one on the bank I promise I won't give a murmur if I don't get another pull before Sunday.'

I settled back on the boat seat to cast down the pool for a third time. As the hours drifted by, I slipped into rumination again. I contemplated the nailed boots of my predecessors through the season; the ducks whirling over-head; the distant chimes of Coldstream's clocks; the wonderful clumps of timber outlined on the Northum-brian hilltops to the south. Brendan mentioned a beat on which two rods took sixty-one salmon a fortnight earlier. Yet for the most part Tweed numbers, like those of almost every river in Scotland, were sadly lagging that year. By telepathy I sought to interrogate my fellow fisher on the beat five hundred yards down the river. Had he caught one, two, three, or none? If he had caught three, what fly was he using? Was his stretch better populated with salmon than mine? Was he casting better than me? Curiosity about our companions' fortunes and, yes, spasms of suspicion and envy, afflict most of us when we are fishing in vain. Lunchtime revealed that my fellow rod had caught one smallish fish. Afternoon brought neither of us luck. Next morning – a beautiful sunny one – found the river up a couple of inches, but nothing was stirring save a horrible red kipper that I embarrassed myself by foul-hooking while casting into fast water under Coldstream bridge. Back into the current it went, amid derisive laughter from the neighbouring beat's boatmen.

On Saturday the river was up fifteen inches, yet surprisingly clean. Only a few leaves and weed knots were drifting down. We started the morning in high hopes. Conditions seemed near perfect. But cast after cast and hour after hour, not only did we not touch a fish, we did not see one. The spate had pushed them upriver. No new shoal had come in. 'Fish on strike, like,' said the Northumbrian boatman laconically. 'Rampant absenteeism,' I suggested. 'They should have a great day on Monday.' I felt no resentment. I had had my turn, a marvellous turn, on Thursday morning. I still savoured the memory of that beautiful fish. With the dearth of water and salmon which prevailed north of the border that season, I was content with the happiness of the place and the experience. I know that as long as even those priceless nuggets of success are still to be gleaned there, I shall go back.

18

Pheasants

$\mathcal{O}$NCE UPON A time the pheasant was an honoured bird, and not only by women who stuck its feathers in their hats. Until late Victorian times, sightings were uncommon enough for its gaudy plumage to rouse oohs and aahs. It remained less important, however, to country sport than its feathered brethren. Trollope's squires talked a lot about their partridges and grouse, rather less about their pheasants. Then came driven game-shooting in the late nineteenth century. Sportsmen perceived the pheasant's utility. It is a heavy, lazy bird which accelerates upwards for a maximum of eight seconds, flies strongly for a while, then settles again. It is much more predictable and manageable than the grouse or partridge, does not stray far, and can be reared in large numbers.

When electric incubators succeeded broody hen coops, the pheasant entered the age of mass production. Today, we take it for granted. It has become a sporting commodity, sold by the hundred, shot by the million every season. The taste police tremble at the vulgarity of its colours. It employs the same couturier as the late Barbara Cartland. It is cursed with the silly eyes of a Church of England vicar cornered at a cocktail party and asked what he thinks about homosexuality. It makes the sort of parent who is always in trouble with Social Services. When it reaches the table my children revolt and say: 'Why can't we have chicken?'

That is the case for the prosecution. Yet stop a moment, and think where field sports would be today without the pheasant. Grouse are caviar, and cost about the same. The wild partridge has become an endangered species. His reared brethren are a joy to meet on a shooting day if they are flying high. But the pheasant has become the staple of English shooting sport – a supremely reliable, almost all-weather performer, at its best superbly exciting and testing. Grouse and partridges thrill us in coveys. We remember wonderful days, great drives. Yet the best pheasants stick in our memories as individuals, whether we hit or missed them. I think of a bird climbing on oxygen alone over the line, in Surrey of all places, twenty-five years ago. There were catcalls from my neighbours as it headed unerringly for me. I raised the gun conscious of forty-odd spectators, from the beaters to the pickers-up

– and killed it. 'My money was on the pheasant,' said a friend sardonically, indeed almost crossly. But of course I was in heaven for five minutes. I haven't forgotten a detail of the occasion, even after all this time.

Likewise, painful details of a mirror incident in Wiltshire a decade later remain etched on my mind. I did not drop the bird. Assorted dukes, crack shots and celebs, none of whom I knew well, roared in delight. I was sure that I had touched that pheasant with the left barrel as it went away. Had I been granted licence, I would have spent an hour with my dog looking for it. I cared that much.

When packs of driven birds come over the guns, often they are visible only as shapes silhouetted against the sky. But to a rough shooter, each flushing pheasant represents a special moment to be cherished. In my twenties, I used to lope at a trot along Midlands hedges, a length behind my questing labrador and two lengths behind a sprinting bird, praying that it would rise on my side and within shot. Say what you will, a low crossing pheasant at thirty yards is much more difficult than even a pretty high driven bird, especially if one is puffing and panting fit to burst. I seldom came home with more than one in the gamebag. Yet for me, that was cause enough for celebration.

Some people like to see pheasants in the garden. Those of us who cherish our borders would rather watch them feeding in the fields with the sun lighting up the cocks' colours, or mushing their tracks in fresh snow. When we lived in Ireland, where pheasants were rare things coveted by members of every local gun club, a roving shooter would follow a bird's marks all morning if he thought there was a chance of a shot. And if he caught the bird, he would more often stuff it than eat it. The shelves of our local taxidermist were lined with pheasants sent to be set up by proud sportsmen. Snipe and pigeon interested them very little. For a pheasant, however, they would ford streams, brave bogs and plunge through brambles.

Half a century ago, shooters used to say: 'Up goes a pound, bang goes sixpence, down comes half a crown.' Today, all those numbers have multiplied many times, save the last. Yet, measured against incomes, both live pheasants and cartridges have become much cheaper. And as for dead birds – we all see how many guns are unwilling to take their brace home. I preach the gospel of the casserole. It is the bones and sinews that can make a pheasant so tiresome on a plate. Braise it, carve the breasts free of every impediment, add cream, apple, celery, Madeira or Calvados, and return to the stove for a while. You have a dish fit for any dinner party, and you are doing your bit to preserve a vital principle of field sports, by eating what you kill.

The pheasant we all admire most is the one we never get to see over the guns, the bird Patrick Chalmers was thinking of when he wrote about the Christmas variety: 'A sage of fourth season, he knows the red reason/for sticks in the covert and "stops" in the strips/and back through the beaters he'll modestly slip.' Pheasants appear at their most winning when they squat looking nervously back over their shoulders, knowing they have been spotted. Then they scuttle away through the long grass with a low, creeping stride like that of Groucho Marx on an off day. Those are the ones which I hope get away, and usually do. Granted, the pheasant is a bit of a spiv. He lacks the honest yeoman qualities of the grey partridge, the Highland pedigree of a grouse. But our winter sporting days would be lost without him. Any shoot is the poorer that treats him simply as an industrial commodity.

19

The English and the Scots

In November 2003 I was invited to give a lecture on behalf of the Scottish National Trust, about the state of the Union between England and Scotland, whose future has come to seem increasingly uncertain over the past thirty years. The Scottish experience means so much to so many English country-dwellers, and the issues of land reform and ownership are so significant, that it seems worth reproducing in this collection an abridged and updated version of that lecture, if only to feed a debate that is likely to remain intensely sensitive through the years ahead.

An English courtier, Sir Anthony Weldon, reported biliously on his experience in Scotland in 1617: 'There is great store of fowl, too, as foul houses, foul sheets, foul linen, foul dishes and pots, foul trenchers and napkins.' For most of their history, the Scots have been defending themselves against such horrid neighbourly condescensions. When that likeable Aberdeenshire lawyer Sir James

Craig came south with James VI and I in 1603, he sought to correct the jaundiced English image of his homeland: 'There is no country in which a man can live more pleasantly and delicately than Scotland. Nowhere else are fish so plentiful; indeed, unless they are freshly caught on the very day we refuse to eat them. There is meat of every kind. Nowhere else will you will find more tender beef and mutton ... our servants are content with oatmeal, which makes them hardy.' Sir John Sinclair of Ulbster, two centuries later, wrote just a trifle defensively: 'Scotland is naturally possessed of some advantages ... any adverse circumstances in its natural situation have tended only to rouse the energies, and stimulate the industry of its inhabitants, who have thence been led to make the greater exertions, in order to overcome these difficulties and to counteract the injurious effects of a northern latitude, a moist and variable climate, and a surface, the greater proportion of which is barren, rocky, and irregular.'

For those of us who love that 'barren, rocky and irregular' land, the first decade of the twenty-first century – four hundred years after the conjunction of the English and Scottish crowns – is not an easy time. Until as recently as thirty years ago, it seemed unthinkable that two nations whose fortunes have been so closely entwined as those of England and Scotland might in our lifetimes be split asunder. We took the Union of England and Scotland as much for granted as winter rain. Yet today we find both assumptions thrown into question, the one by global warming, the other by social, economic and political tensions.

I am an Englishman with, so far as I know, no drop of Scottish blood in my veins. Yet all my life I have cherished a passion for Scotland, its culture and history, its people and landscape. My father, strongly influenced by his sporting enthusiasms, was accustomed to speak of the northern nation of the United Kingdom with reverence. He called the Highlands 'God's country', and he instilled this creed in me. I love the cadences of Scots accents of various hues almost as dearly as the skirl of the pipes. Every year for four decades, I have spent idyllic days casting flies on Scottish rivers, or walking with a gun over Scottish hills. In the eyes of some Scots today, such enthusiasms make me the sort of visitor to their country who raises their hackles. I would make matters worse if I mentioned that when I was twenty-five I came within an ace of wearing the kilt on Scottish holidays, until the unrestrained mockery of friends dissuaded me.

Thus, however clumsy my embraces, I have enjoyed a romance with Scotland all my life, from days when my father sent me to hand-milk cows on a small farm in Inverness-shire in school holidays. This makes me one of those Englishmen who care deeply about all that happens north of the border, and especially to lament the stresses in the modern relationship between the two nations. In 1996 I wrote a magazine article asserting that we, the English, should recognise how much we are disliked by some Scots. The Scottish press picked this up on a slow news day, and prominently advertised it as an attack on the Scots, which it certainly was not intended to be. My own friends with Scottish connections received the piece with a mixture of scorn, irritation and disbelief. Most asserted that what I said was untrue; some said that even if my thesis was valid, it was unhelpful to acknowledge it in public.

Yet I believed then, and still do so now, that only by confronting disagreeable issues can we hope to come to terms with them. Today, there is little cause to retreat from what I wrote in 1996. Scottish hostility towards the English displays itself with a vigour that deeply dismays many people on both sides of the border. More than a few sportsmen travelling north encounter undertones of hostility in some local communities. A significant force in the migration of English sportsmen to Alaska, Iceland and suchlike is that they can be much more confident of a warm welcome. Not long ago, I heard a young man in a Highland village say wonderingly: 'I see people in the pub on Saturday night who want to go out and *fight* the English.' Casual abuse of southern neighbours in the Scottish media and the Edinburgh Parliament is a commonplace. The British Army has been shocked to perceive widespread resentment north of the border about the deployment of Scottish regiments in Iraq. This was seen by some Scots as bitter fruit of an English decision to support an American war, in which it was wrong to expect sons of Scotland to risk their lives. Since 1976, Scottish football crowds have sung 'Flower of Scotland' rather than 'God Save the Queen' before international matches. Forty per cent of Scottish respondents told pollsters that they would prefer any other team before England to win the last European Cup. Even if this sort of thing reflects the crudest aspect of popular senti-ment, there is plenty of anecdotal evidence to confirm its pervasiveness. What has generated this new mood among significant numbers of people north of the border?

At the heart of the matter, surely, is the difficulty which afflicts almost all strained marriages. One or other party finds their self-esteem, their sense of self-worth, so injured that anger and resentment break forth. The apportionment of fault is less important, at first anyway, than acknowledging the reality of the condition. For at least the past three decades, many Scottish people – for some reasons that may justly be blamed upon the English, and for others which may not – have found it hard to feel good about themselves; this despite a notable revival of Scottish culture, and a Scottish ministerial dominance of Britain's government that makes the English sometimes feel mere colonial subjects. Historian Richard Weight, author of a penetrating recent study of nationalism, is among those who perceive a strand of self-hatred in the extremes of modern Scottish behaviour, vividly reflected in the monologue of Renton, one of the junkies in the 1996 film *Trainspotting*. Renton breaks forth into a cry of anguish: 'I hate being Scottish. We're the lowest of the fucking low, the scum of the earth, the most wretched, servile, miserable, pathetic trash that ever shat into civilisation. Some people hate the English, but I don't. They're just wankers. We, on the other hand, are colonised by wankers. We can't even pick a decent culture to be colonised by.' This is a voice of the underclass. But it would be foolish not to recognise its authenticity, the pessimism and even despair that have become tragic forces in many Scottish urban communities. Alienation towards the English has mounted since at least the 1970s.

It persists to this day, and of course has its roots in history.

Almost a hundred years after the 1707 abolition of the Scottish Parliament, at the end of the eighteenth century, the Scots began to reap dramatic economic benefits from the Union of their kingdom with that of England. The coming of the Industrial Revolution, followed by improvements in communication made possible by steam, gave Scotland take-off, a remarkable new prosperity, and a matching cultural revival, exemplified by the birth of the *Edinburgh Review* in 1802 and the *Scotsman* in 1817, together with the burgeoning international fame first of Burns and Adam Smith, then of Scott. The English, who for centuries had looked upon the northern kingdom as a barbarous land rich chiefly in rebels, suddenly discovered a respect for Scotland's beauty, industry, culture and commercial talents which grew throughout the nineteenth century. George IV's visit to Edinburgh in 1822 set the seal upon a growing love affair, deepened by the Caledonian passions of the Royal Family.

Neither Walter Scott nor later distinguished compatriots such as John Buchan saw any contradiction between being Scottish and being British. They were proud to be both. The British Empire, in the creation and management of which the Scots played so prominent a part, provided a conspicuous rationale for Union. Thinking Scots recognised that the Empire offered them opportunities alongside the English which they would never have enjoyed alone. Thinking Englishmen, in their turn, respected the genius which Scots displayed to such effect across every continent, as soldiers, engineers and entrepreneurs. It became impossible to think of the British Army without its Scottish regiments, to imagine the Empire's trade without its Scottish houses, to envisage any landscape ruled by Britain without its bridges and railways created by Scots. The nineteenth century witnessed an extraordinary lifting of the Scottish condition. One historian has written: 'In the place of passive resignation to poverty, there was a lightening of the spirit that showed through every aspect of Scottish life and culture.'

Yet it is impossible to speak of Scotland in the nineteenth century without mentioning its darkest face, which has coloured the view of posterity, and of the Scots themselves, out of all proportion to the numbers of people involved. The Highland Clearances, the forcible removal of clansmen and their families from the lands they tenanted, on a road that led most to emigration, while the glens they quit were repopulated by sheep, were most vigorously executed in Sutherland. It could scarcely fail to seem a bitter matter that tens of thousands of people were driven against their will from land their ancestors had occupied for centuries. In some areas the policy was especially brutally executed, notoriously in those controlled by Patrick Sellar, the Sutherland family factor who cleared Strathnaver in 1814. Strathnaver became, and has remained, the epicentre of Highland grievances towards lairds and lords. The wrath of the dispossessed clansmen was fuelled by a stonemason named Donald Macleod, who from exile in Canada sustained a torrent of polemic and propaganda against the Sutherland family for forty years after the Clearances ended, and provided a basis for John Prebble's impressively impassioned view of the story, published 150 years later. The Clearances were the responsibility of Scottish landlords, but bitter Highlanders attributed this betrayal to the degree to which clan chiefs had allowed themselves to assimilate with the English nobility and with English greed and manners.

Nothing can diminish posterity's revulsion against the Highland evictions. They can, however, be set in context. Whatever solution was adopted, by the nineteenth century the Highlands had become incapable of sustaining their population, which had increased dramatically over two or three generations. The lives of many clansmen were unspeakably miserable, certainly no rural idyll. T. C. Smout has written: 'Nothing could be more misplaced than the glamour with which the fanciful have sometimes invested Highland society before the "45".' In 1772 an English visitor, Thomas Pennant, described the people of the Highlands as 'almost torpid with idleness, and most wretched; their hovels most miserable . . . There is not corn raised sufficient to supply half the wants of the inhabitants . . . Numbers of the miserables of this country were now migrating; they wandered in a state of desperation; too poor to pay, they madly sell themselves for their passage, preferring a temporary bondage in a strange land to starving for life in their native soil.' Many local Highland landowners behaved with ruthless selfishness towards their own people. Macdonald of Clanranald, for instance, received the enormous income of £17,000 a year from rents and kelp on South Uist, but spent almost all of this on his own pleasures, with small attempt to relieve the distress of tenants on his acres which, like most of the Highlands and Islands, were wretchedly overcrowded.

By contrast, the Sutherland family has received less

credit than is its due for the efforts made by its chiefs in the nineteenth century to improve the economy of their vast lands – building roads, farms, steadings, model industries and model fishing harbours such as Helmsdale. Paternalistic the Sutherlands may have been, and in some respects brutally insensitive. But their efforts to establish textile working and fisheries, to raise their people from poverty, were well-intentioned and honourable. Because these attempts failed, partly owing to a national economic downturn, the family is remembered only for its evictions. What is certain, however, is that with or without the Clearances, the old hill life in Sutherland and elsewhere was doomed. The clans constituted military societies. Once local strife and cattle raiding ceased, the clan system was bound to atrophy, and should not be idealised.

Richard Weight sets the Clearances in a wider historical context: 'Although Scotland had a generally lower standard of living than England and Wales, the Union benefited the Scots throughout its three-hundred-year history. Had it not occurred, Scotland (like its partners) would have been poorer, her Enlightenment less vigorous, her industrial revolution slower and her empire less extensive. With the exception of the Highland Clearances, ordinary Scots endured no major injustice that the English did not also endure between 1707 and 2000. No meaningful comparison can therefore be made with the Irish experience of union, in which millions were starved and killed.'

In the nineteenth century the Highlands became chiefly known to English tourists as a paradise for sportsmen and admirers of natural beauty, unsullied by much human activity save that associated with sport. Smout again: 'The habit of assuming that the Highlanders were congenitally incapable of any effort or self-help had been ingrained in upper-class Scottish thinking since the days of James VI.' For many modern Scots, the sight of the empty glens is less an advertisement for nature than a memorial to the hapless clansmen who were driven from them. This view may be irrational and overstated. But it would be foolish to doubt the power of the image among a new generation, educated to a partisan and often woefully misleading view of history – what we might call the Braveheart culture. This is intensified by some local 'heritage centres' in the Highlands, which today perpetuate a wildly fanciful view of old grievances.

The corrosion of Scotland's prosperity and self-confidence began in the years between the two world wars. The country experienced a short-lived resurgence between 1939 and 1945, but thereafter its fortunes declined steadily. Traditional heavy industries, which had made the country great for almost two centuries – coal, steel and shipbuilding – found themselves drifting towards extinction. Despite considerable efforts by successive Westminster governments, no new Scottish enterprises came close to matching the wealth-generating powers of those that disappeared. The Empire, which had provided extraordinary opportunity for Scots to prosper beneath the Union flag, was put into receivership. Beyond a sense of national impoverishment, Scots felt the deep pain of fallen pride. In the last thirty years of the twentieth century, these sentiments went further. They grew into an anger towards their southern neighbours and the government far away at Westminster. The English seemed indifferent to Scotland's misfortunes, which in some regions became human tragedies.

The resurgence of Scottish nationalism, which began in a very modest fashion in the 1960s, gathered pace amid Scotland's economic woes of the 1980s and 1990s. Even among those who had no wish for outright independence, a desire grew for devolved government, for Scotland's right in some degree to manage its own affairs. The English seemed to have failed the country. Westminster appeared intolerably remote. Yet since the creation of the Scottish Parliament in 1999, many Scots have suffered disillusionment. The horrendous bill for the Edinburgh Parliament building has become a symbol of the Scottish executive's incompetence and profligacy. Scottish voters vent their disappointment, to anyone who will listen, that so little of tangible benefit to the country has so far emerged from the experiment in self-government. The Parliament's most headline-catching acts have been gestures to address historic resentments against the old ruling class – a ban on fox-hunting and the introduction of land reform – rather than measures which seek to take Scotland forward in the twenty-first century. The proposal, seriously considered by MSPs, to impose sanctions upon any Scottish pub or restaurant which failed to allow breastfeeding in public, did almost as much damage to the image of the institution abroad as the chronic corruption within the Scottish Labour Party. The behaviour of MSPs, the 'McPygmies' as some English newspapers styled them, has prompted widespread derision in the south. In an age when political parties throughout Britain are dismayed by the poor quality of candidates willing to offer themselves for public service, this problem is especially evident in the first generation of MSPs.

Scotland's economic fortunes will always be determined by what happens in the Central Belt, focus of population and economic activity. Statistically, the fate of the Highlands is marginal. Yet Scotland's wildernesses exercise a symbolic influence, and occupy an emotional place in national thinking, out of all proportion to the numbers of people who inhabit them. The Scottish Parliament devoted immense time and energy to the Land Reform Act which was finally passed in 2002. This grants local communities a right to buy estates which are offered for sale; gives unlimited public access by day and night to almost all private land; and offers crofting tenants rights to buy into fisheries adjoining the land they occupy. The economic importance of land reform is negligible, and the number of people directly affected is small, at least in the short term. Yet it possesses immense symbolic significance in the minds of those who perceive Scotland's history as a story of English exploitation and condescension. The land reform controversy brings together two intensely emotional issues – alleged historic misappropriation of peasant lands, and a class-based hostility to field sports. There is an instinctive distaste in some circles for anything that smacks of what used to be called a 'toff', and of the traditional pleasures of 'toffs'. There is a gut dislike of the fact that large areas of the Highland landscape are owned by rich outsiders who shoot, fish or stalk there.

This sentiment was vividly expressed in an influential

book entitled *Who Owns Scotland?*, written by an angry young man named Andy Wightman and published in Edinburgh in 1996. Wightman wrote: 'The sporting estate in reality is an indulgence by wealthy people who like hunting. They are uneconomic because they were never designed to be economic. No rural development programme anywhere in the world advocates the sale of land to a few wealthy individuals who will then support the rural economy by injecting cash from outside which will in turn support a few jobs . . . As James Hunter recently observed when it was suggested that landowners might feel threatened by the developing debate about land ownership: "The more they feel threatened in my view the better. They need to feel threatened and they should feel threatened because there can be no future in Britain in the twenty-first century for a rural economy dependent on tweedy gentlemen coming from the south to slaughter our wildlife."'

Wightman blames the situation in which only sporting uses are self-financing on 'lack of investment in productive land uses and enterprises . . . compounded by the narrow outlook of successive proprietors'. He argues that 'much of the poor land in Scotland is poor not solely through inherent constraints such as soil quality and climate but as a result of abuse and failure to exploit its full potential'. This is hard to swallow. Throughout history, some good men and some rich men and many public bodies have poured money into efforts to galvanise northern Scotland. They failed not because goodwill or money were lacking, but because, contrary to the beliefs of such zealots as Wightman and Hunter, it is incredibly difficult to make things work or pay in Britain's remote wildernesses. Field sports are the only activities which are self-sustaining, environmentally friendly, and funded through the enthusiasms of rich proprietors, some of them genuinely philanthropic.

The land reformers are socialists of the purest kind, because they assume an almost infinite willingness by the state to fund utopia. Their belief in community ownership flies in the face of historic experience, and of the reality that almost nowhere in Europe is small farming a viable activity without public subsidy. It may be argued that Scottish eagerness to dispossess large landowners merely matches the successful spirit of the campaign for tenants' rights in Ireland more than a century ago. Yet the land at issue in the Irish reform process was tillage, ground worked for corn and potatoes, or grazed by cattle. The land which interests Scottish reformers today offers no possibility of yielding profit, save through agricultural subsidy.

Most of the fishings which come within the horizons of the Reform Act require relentless financial support from their owners, rather than yielding profit. The few angling properties which have so far fallen into community ownership are languishing. The world has moved far since the Highland Clearances, or even since Irish land reform. The Irish process was designed to provide a new economic dispensation for an agricultural people. Scotland is no longer an agricultural society. Moreover, the measures in the Land Reform Act to provide public access to privately-owned lands are so far-reaching that it is plain their purpose is to punish the private landowner, rather than to profit the citizen with wanderlust.

Almost the only genuinely self-sustaining activities in many Highland areas are field sports. Rich proprietors and visitors are willing to pay large sums to shoot grouse, stalk deer or catch salmon. Far from exploiting Scottish natural resources to achieve profit, such people are subsidising jobs and the environment on a substantial scale. Very few landowners make money, even where they let their sport to tenants. Four estates in the Tomatin area, typical of their kind, opened their books to public inspection in 1999, as part of an effort to induce politicians and the public to adopt a more rational view of the Highland economy. Those accounts showed that, on average, each owner was subsidising his property to the tune of around £100,000 a year. If such estates ever fall into public ownership, or are diverted to local communities, not only will the cash injections of rich proprietors be lost, but subsidy will be required from the public purse to replace them. It was dismaying that on this issue the Edinburgh Parliament showed a determination to ignore submissions of evidence from landowners, sometimes with studied rudeness, and to act on the basis of gut sentiment of a primitive socialist kind. The Land Reform Act amounted to a declaration of war on landowning interests, and indeed on field sports.

While the legislation attracted bitter criticism from the sporting community and thousands of people employed on moors, forests and rivers, it was passed with little noise from anybody else up north. Scots seemed chiefly preoccupied with the folk memory of the Clearances. The Act was supported by some militant Highland-dwellers – more than a few of them 'incomers' without a drop of

Scottish blood in their veins – and of course by the viscerally nationalist Scottish media. Even if many Scots did not enthuse about the new law – 'Mugabe in a kilt', in the vivid phrase of a *Daily Telegraph* writer – few openly opposed it. The revival of rural communities is an article of faith. Land reform is presented to Scots in seductively simple terms: Surely it must be in the interests of the Highlands if millions of acres now occupied by a few rich landowners, devoted to snobbish and bloodstained pastimes, are replaced by larger numbers of smallholders, engaged in more innocent activities?

It was saddening to hear the head of a powerful English rural quango declare recently: 'We should recognise that land is always better managed in public ownership.' Such sentiment is amazingly widespread. It is ironic that it should be so, when around the world public stewardship of property has become discredited. It is dismaying that such agencies as Scottish National Heritage and the Deer Commission sometimes give the impression of pursuing an agenda designed to fit that of the Scottish Parliament, and echoing its distaste for traditional private landowners, rather than adopting policies based on objective, independent consideration of the environment and public interest. A long, painful task lies ahead, to convince the old-fashioned collectivists that they are wrong. If their reasoning prevails, we shall end up living in a vast suburbia interrupted only by a few densely-regulated national parks, to remind us what our countryside once was. This is a problem for England, but a much graver one for Scotland.

I have searched my conscience about my own behaviour

as a visitor to the Highlands. Like many another eager English sportsman, I suspect that in the past I overdid it, revelling in the fun of playing laird-by-rental. Yet if some sporting activities in the Highlands represent a charade staged by 'Piccadilly Highlanders', it seems a harmless one, which has brought a great deal of money to the north. The behaviour of the Scottish Parliament is self-indulgent. Its message is that Scotland is willing to forgo a large income from foreign sportsmen, and even to provide public money to subsidise uneconomic crofting activity as a substitute, for the pleasure of assaulting a landowning and sporting life that offends Central Belt sensibilities. English taxpayers will some day wake up to the fact that money, much of which ultimately comes from their pockets, is being employed to fund an exercise in Scottish social engineering.

Despite the contrary claims of Messrs Wightman, Hunter and others, it is impossible to imagine any transfer of land to local communities, or shift of purpose from sporting to other agricultural or commercial activities, which will offer a prospect of viability, or of providing comparable employment. Nor is it always possible to take at face value the militancy of some local Highland communities. The most strident opponents of traditional ownership are often incomers who buy crofts merely as holiday or retirement properties. A friend who lives on an estate in the north and finds himself at odds with some of his tenants about crofting rights describes himself, not unjustly, as a resident landlord litigating with absentee crofters. A parallel with Irish experience may be recognised. For at least half a century after independence in

1922, the land policies of successive Irish governments were driven overwhelmingly by a determination to distance themselves from the English, and where possible to spite them. Only in the past thirty years has the Dáil in Dublin belatedly adopted some rational environmental and conservation policies, after decades in which Irishmen asserted a determination to flaunt their freedom from landlord rule at any cost, even to their own landscape and fisheries.

I remain optimistic that the Scottish Parliament will eventually grow into its role, though its political adolescence may continue for some years to be as painful for the Scottish people as for concerned onlookers. The practical damage done by the Land Reform Act, the scale of take-up by local communities, may turn out to be far more modest than prophets of doom fear. There is absolutely no reason to oppose the notion of local people buying land when it is offered for sale, if they can financially sustain both the purchase and subsequent management. The objection must be to the diversion of public money to fund social engineering, in the hope of undoing perceived consequences of the Clearances two centuries ago.

For the sake of both Scotland and England, we should hope that the learning curve of the Edinburgh legislature is far steeper than was that of Ireland after its independence. No one should blame Scottish politicians for acting in support of their own interests, asserting their own nationhood and culture. The challenge is to resist a temptation to indulge mere spleen against the English, in a fashion which must harm the Scottish people themselves. It seems a somewhat limited social ambition, in the twenty-first century, to seek through public subsidy to restore a peasant class to the Highlands.

The English response to devolution, and to Scottish hostility, has thus far been remarkably muted. There has been growing publicity about the much larger per capita slice of public spending which the Scots receive over the English. The fact that Scotland has become overwhelmingly the political territory of the Labour Party, the Liberal Democrats and the Nationalists has caused some Conservatives to consider turning their faces away from the northern kingdom altogether, in pursuit of political and economic advantage. They argue that Scottish, and thus English, independence would be of real benefit to southern taxpayers, who would no longer have to pay the bills for Scotland, and to the Conservative Party, which at a stroke could cut loose scores of constituencies which are unlikely ever again to endorse its claims to power. They fantasise about thus creating an almost permanent Tory majority in an English House of Commons. By a bizarre twist, a community of sentiment has thus evolved between Scottish nationalists and some Tory zealots.

The English right-wing vision seems misplaced. I remember a Tory Cabinet minister remarking fifteen years ago that he believed the separation of Scotland and England would diminish both nations more than either recognises, and more than any raw economic calculation might suggest. This seems just. It is surely significant that some European nations, notably the French, regard a partition of Scotland and England with enthusiasm, precisely because they believe that it would diminish the voice of both nations in the European Union.

Yet some thoughtful observers believe that, sooner or later, Scottish independence is likely, if not inevitable. Norman Davies, in his recent book *The Isles*, reminded us how relatively brief is the history of the United Kingdom. He suggested that its dissolution is inevitable in a new world in which the advantages of the Union seem much less plain than once they did, and in which the independence of minorities within the wider entity of Europe is being pursued by many national groups. Richard Weight suggests that the Scots will continue to hover on the brink of secession, while finally flinching from adopting this option because they do not wish to pay for it. Yet Weight also argues that the loss of Empire, the fading of the memory of the Second World War as a unifying force, together with decline in public enthusiasm for the shared monarchy, and increasing blurring of British national identity in Europe, make the Union's long-term future seem doubtful. He suggests that it would be rash to believe that it can survive for more than a century, if that.

In looking to the future, we should return to the issue I raised above – that of self-esteem. Today, for a variety of reasons, some of which are their own fault and some not, many Scots do not feel good about themselves. If they were more self-confident of their own status and identity, they might enjoy a much more comfortable relationship with the English. Because our nation is overwhelmingly the larger and richer partner, the chief responsibility must fall upon England, to work harder to demonstrate respect for Scottish sensitivities and to boost Scottish self-regard. That penetrating historian Linda Colley told a Downing Street conference in 1999: 'Instead of being mesmerised by debates over British identity, it would be far more productive to concentrate on renovating British citizenship, and on convincing all of the inhabitants of these islands that they are equal and valued citizens irrespective or whatever identity they may individually select to prioritise.' In other words, it is scarcely surprising that some Scots choose to think little of their British status when many of the English seem to regard their Celtic extremities with condescension.

Conversely, Scottish comedian Billy Connolly expresses contempt for his own people's nationalism with a vigour which strikes a chord with many English people. He identifies 'a new Scottish racism, which I loathe – this thing that everything horrible is English'. It is striking that while Scottish accents prosper mightily on England's broadcast airwaves, it is impossible to imagine an English accent being welcome on most radio or television stations in the north. A while ago I heard a senior member of the Bush administration, Bob Zoellick, complain that Europe's foremost, if not only, way to express its own identity appears to be in terms of a determination to distance itself from things American. It might be argued that Scots likewise find it much easier to define themselves through hostility to things English than through a positive vision of their own situation and destiny. If they felt more comfortable with themselves, they might feel less confrontational towards England.

To sustain the Union over the next century, it will be

necessary for both nations to perceive its practical advantages more clearly, and for the English to display generosity, even in the face of continuing provocation from Scottish politicians and the Scottish media. Only if the Scots recover their faith in themselves as respected partners, rather than as despised dependants, can the settlement hope to survive. This can only be achieved if they and their Parliament prove capable of a better understanding of the disciplines indispensable to twenty-first-century commerce and enterprise than they have displayed in the recent past. In the short term, nationalists are on the defensive because of the visible shortcomings of Scottish self-governance. In a few years, however, the forces for independence will rise again, if Scots feel themselves failing under the Union flag.

It is dismaying that, partly because of the limitations of the Scottish media, debate north of the border about the merits and limitations of the Union is cheap and strident. Walter Scott's fictional Bailie Jarvie in 1715 rebuked one of his fellow-countrymen for abusing the English in terms that might readily be applied to today's Scottish media: 'It's ill-scraped tongues like yours that make mischief atween neighbours and nations.' Too many thoughtful people in the north, who should be speaking out publicly about the rational case for Union – so much stronger from a Scottish viewpoint than an English one – are reluctant to raise their voices against the fashionable nationalist mood.

In suggesting that we, the English, need to work harder at assisting the revival of Scottish self-worth, I do not suggest that we must accept every argument on Scottish terms. It is one thing to recognise that some Scots are irked by tweedy Englishmen shooting on their hills. It is quite another to bow to the dotty pastoral visions and shameless class-warrior spirit of such campaigners as Andy Wightman. It is one thing to ask the English to accept that if we want the Union to survive, we must fund more infrastructure in Scotland. It is another, however, to expect English voters to swallow violent expressions of Scottish antipathy even as they pay the bills to satisfy Scottish ambitions. Scotland must look forward, not back. If the nation should sometime choose the path to independence, it will never receive from the European Union the sort of huge financial hand-outs from which Ireland profited in the 1970s. Today there are simply too many rival contenders for EU largesse. Scots will be rash if they provoke the English too far, by sustaining their abuse of the partner that pays so many bills.

For Englishmen who love Scotland, there is something of the pain of a rejected suitor in perceiving the mood among some Scots towards us. The folly seems self-evident of tormenting rich foreigners – particularly the English – in Scotland. Patience, goodwill, statesmanship, money, and above all a fundamental belief that the preservation of the Union is important to all of us, will be necessary if it is to persist beyond our lifetimes. Even romantic unionists such as myself must concede that, from an English viewpoint, the case for maintaining the link is today chiefly emotional and nostalgic, rather than rational or economic. It is unlikely that there will ever again be a time when Scotland and England cohabit in tranquillity as the two nations did in the palmy years of the nineteenth century. The future relationship will remain chronically restless. The issue of Scottish independence will always be somewhere near the table.

Yet the two nations have shared so much in the past, and continue to share so much to this day. Scotland should be able to forge a future as a centre of twenty-first-century excellence, without the necessity to preserve a reputation, which today's Scottish Parliament sometimes seems to seek, as a retirement home for twentieth-century lost causes. Both nations will be diminished if the people of the northern kingdom finally insist upon going their own way, or provoke English patience beyond endurance. The prize of sustaining the Union seems great enough to deserve generosity of spirit to preserve a marriage which has meant so much to so many of us for so long.

20

A Fishing Party

$\mathscr{I}$ HAVE NEVER worked as a tour guide, but I fancy the experience would be a doddle for anyone who has ever organised a fishing party. As a guest, I marvel at the good nature, generosity and patience of hosts. Why is it that men and women who run their working lives and domestic affairs with a self-discipline that would do credit to a biblical flagellant go to pieces as guests on a sporting holiday? They forget whether they are expected on Sunday or Monday, have been asked to bring ham or cheese, are fishing Beat One or Four.

Then it comes to my turn to lead the band in a lodge. My wife says that I should be more philosophical about who catches what. It is all luck, isn't it? Yet, especially when one has a lot of novices aboard, it is hard not to become obsessed with an ambition to see that everybody goes home with a fish. Monday is always cheerful, because all the week lies ahead. A year or two ago on the Helmsdale, I assured old Charlie that the Short or the Jetties was sure to produce some action, and packed him off as near to 9 a.m. as he could be mobilised. I told Angus, who was gillying, that I would be grovellingly grateful if my own son caught a fish, and dispatched the team with hope in my heart. Amid family teams I do most of my own fishing between six and nine in the morning, and nine and twelve at night, to leave the coast reasonably clear for the young entry. While they are casting, I read an unimproving book.

Though that debut day was blank, Tuesday looked encouraging, because we were fishing more promising water. There was heavy overcast and a strong wind across the stream – better conditions than we had seen in recent sunlit years. By lunchtime, things were looking up. One rod, Peter, had landed two fish, and was ecstatic. Nobody could move anything on the top stretch. That evening in a half-gale, my wife and I flogged the Wash and the run above the Railway Bridge until darkness, achieving nothing more than a couple of swirls at the fly. At the last gasp, I hooked and lost a fish, chiefly because my concentration had flagged.

Next day at nine, I suffered an agony of frustration because my twenty-one year-old son opted for a stint in bed rather than fish one of the best stretches on the river, as I had begged him to do. I grumbled and harangued him a trifle unconvincingly, because I remembered being a bit that way myself at his age. I fished instead, caught two and lost another. All these joys, I told him sternly at lunchtime, would have been his had he not et cetera, et cetera. From the upper beat, we heard a tale of tragedy. James, the son of my fellow-fisher Peter and a newcomer to salmon, lost a fish that was certainly fifteen pounds, maybe seventeen, according to the gillie. An element of what tennis players call unforced error came into the story. But which of us has not done or undone as much? Our guides were uneasy about the shortage of fresh fish in the river. I was selfish enough to wonder why the fish that took James's fly at 11 a.m. in the Gravelly had declined mine in the same pool at seven, but such is life. My son lost a fish that afternoon.

Our other guest was leaving on Wednesday afternoon. In consequence, both of us spent that morning in a fever of anxiety. God was merciful. He landed his fish. I waved him happily off southwards. Peter caught another one, too. But what about the rest of the team? Here we were, more than halfway through the week, and three young fishers – not to mention my wife – had yet to score anything bigger than a parr. Nothing does more to encourage beginners than catching something. I clasped my hands and gazed skywards in supplication. On Thursday afternoon I watched my son and his girlfriend fish down some of the best water on the beat. She lost one, he moved nothing. At 4.30, in flat water at the tail of the Kilpheddir pool, there was a splash around his fly just in front of a big rock. He lifted his rod point and tightened the line. I spent five minutes on my knees on the bank, forcing myself not to speak while George the gillie directed operations. At last George scooped the net, and waved triumphantly aloft a five-pound salmon.

Now, that fish was quite fresh, but it must have been in the river a week. 'How many flies do you think he has seen before he took ours?' mused George wonderingly. I was only grateful. What wonderful moments these are in the lives of every sporting family. If that salmon knew what pleasure he gave to the Hastingses, I am confident that he would not have regretted his fate. I took a grilse that night in the Whinnie, which made me happy – but not as happy as our shared experience at teatime.

Early on Friday morning I cast down one of the less promising stretches of our beat, to pass the time until the young appeared. They were all leaving that day. At 6.30 we put James on the Marrel, while my son's girlfriend fished down the Whinnie, with me poised between the two. I saw James's rod bend, and dashed to his side clutching the net. He did everything right. A few minutes later we landed a grilse. I gave another huge sigh of relief. Ten minutes later, Jane was playing a fish. I splashed through the shallows to stand beside her: 'Don't touch the reel . . . rod point up . . . let him run, let him run! . . . Reel in, reel in!' Her pretty face was locked in concentration and excitement. I put out the net, missed, saw the fish run again, come back – and I had it. I collapsed on the bank, emotionally sated. The young went home embracing their exhilaration, and maybe hooked on salmon fishing.

My wife caught a fish late in the morning. I had a

twelve-pounder under somewhat dubious circumstances at early evening – foul-hooked in heavy water – and on Saturday enjoyed a thrilling chase down the steep Falls pools to land a grilse after a narrow escape from precipitating myself into the torrent. We drove south exhausted, ready for a holiday to recover, as one usually feels after a week like that. If anybody wants me to lead a coach party of alcoholic Marxists for a vacation in Baghdad, I can contemplate the prospect with perfect equanimity. But it might not be such bliss.

21

Rummage in the Gun Cupboard

$\mathcal{L}$IKE MOST PEOPLE who fish or shoot, I have at home a bulging cupboard full of the tools of my pastimes – some bought, some borrowed, some inherited, some left behind by careless guests. Lest anyone think I am a looter, however, I promise that I have left behind vastly more kit in other people's houses than they have endowed us with. One lazy evening, I set about rummaging through the miscellany. First out of the shelves was a packet of sealed plastic bags containing some jellied substance and a lot of Oriental instructions. I seemed to remember that these were hand-warmers, brought to me by a friend as a present from Japan a few years ago. I could never get those jellies to warm, however often I shoved them into ovens, fridges, microwaves. Time to chuck them away. But then again, perhaps not. Who knows when Arctic winters will descend on Britain again, and we might need them?

Anyway, the hand-warmers got me started on a proper

clear-out of the cupboard, something I have not done for years. What an odd and often embarrassing business it is, going through old gear. It is so healthy and bracing to purge all the redundant bits. What have we here? Two tins of percussion caps which my father used during his muzzle-loading phase. I shall never have the nerve to fire his old Mantons. What could I need percussion caps for? Yet I could not bring myself to bin them. Then there was a stack of beautiful black-enamelled metal boxes, containing old fishing tackle. I bought a lot of spinning gear twenty-something years ago when we lived in Ireland, used it for a while, then decided that throwing a bait is boring. I have never touched a Mepps or a Devon since, but a score of them survive in my cupboard. Then there were some old cast tins of my father's, dating from the days when gut leaders had to be meticulously dried and nurtured. I found myself gazing upon Amadou and Mucilin, split shot and prawning tackle, together with a lump of lead that must weigh north of three pounds. Underneath these objects were two very, very old jars of something called Motty Rifle Paste. What, for God's sake, is rifle paste?

I pulled out a jumble of cable tied up with a cartridge extractor, to reveal the electric welly driers that seemed such a good idea when glimpsed in a mail-order catalogue ten years ago. I have used them once. There was a stack of flasks, several handsome and silver-mounted. Yet most hosts nowadays provide a communal sharpener on shooting mornings, and recent seasons have been far too mild to justify recourse to the bottle. There were two old rifle 'scopes, dismounted when I bought new and improved models under the delusion that they would make me shoot straighter.

What have we here? A pistol-cleaning rod. You couldn't get more redundant than that, since successive governments ruthlessly purged sporting pistols. Oh yes, and a pair of Burberry's canvas gaiters of the kind favoured by officers in Flanders circa 1917, which are too small for my huge feet; a camouflage pigeon mask, in which at the age of ten I fancied myself the Lone Ranger; an assortment of spur straps, mysteriously detached from the spurs; and a duck call, which friends persuaded me to abandon on the grounds that on my lips it was great for conservation, rather less helpful to the bag.

What would I be offered for Lot 777, a Webley target launcher, designed to project empty tins propelled by a .22 blank? The targets never went very far or high at the best of times, and since manufacturers changed the shape of beer cans I have been unable to make them go any-where at all. Then come three old leather cartridge belts, with several loops broken. These must have been in the family sixty years. How many belts can a man need, at least since I left behind the teenage days when I liked to dress for shooting in the manner of Pancho Villa, with two slung across my chest? Beyond lay a great stack of cardboard .22 targets. I only call upon these once a year, when I take a vow to make better practice at vermin.

Beneath this lot lay a ferret line, nets and a ferret collar

– another of father's old enthusiasms, which somehow I have never got into. I also found a spent heavy-calibre rifle bullet which he dug out of some vast African animal he extinguished, together with a rather smaller one that Duff Hart-Davis embarrassingly extracted from the carcass of a stag I had shot twenty years ago, embedded in its spine two feet above my aiming point. I remember the bemused Duff demanding as he probed in vain for the projectile in all the proper places: 'Tell me, Hastings, did this beast simply die of fright?'

Beside my gamebook in the cupboard languished an old leather fly book, once crammed with huge old gut-tied flies, most of which I have removed for mounting, for I shall never fish with them. The words 'Dr Milligan, Ligoniel, Belfast' were indelibly penned on the inside flap, I would guess a century ago. Tucked beside that inscription is a sheaf of jungle-cock feathers which father acquired at gunpoint in India, to tie his sea-trout flies. Odd flies, of course, are littered all over my cupboard, as they are in the treasure chests of every fisherman. Most are quite unsuitable for catching fish, but I can't bring myself to throw them out.

Next comes a neatly partitioned flat wooden box that will never be used again, for it is designed to house a birds' egg collection. My father was an eager collector, and tried to get me interested as a child. Sure enough, I loved discovering nests, but my heart was never in taking and blowing eggs. Beyond that fragment of ornithological history is a beautiful big japanned box full of half-century old dry flies, each pattern beneath its spring-loaded lid. It would be sacrilegious to take them to the river nowadays, but I love to look on them. There is also a round steel counter – an old Norfolk Liar – which I have never used. I have enough trouble hitting things at driven shoots without trying to click a clock every time as well.

Phew. Surveying the debris, it was easy to see how easy it would be to make more space at Hastings Towers by doing away with the whole lot. I should be honest, however. None of that collection has quite yet found its way to the dustbin, or even to a saleroom. One of these days I promise myself that I will do the sensible thing, and empty the cupboard. Or if not, at least I will try to explain to myself why I love all that ancestral clutter so much, and cannot bear to part with any of it.

22

Rough and Smooth in Cornwall

A CORNISH WRITER observed back in 1930: 'The first advice I should give anyone visiting Cornwall for the first time is that he should take her for an island; and the second, for a recently discovered one.' In the same vein, a geographer of the first Elizabeth's reign described the county as 'a foreign country on that side of England nearest Spain'. Like all the extremities of Britain, Cornwall today remains a sportsman's paradise, offering the sort of experiences that have become hard to come by amid what passes for civilisation in the middle bits of these islands. There is wonderful rough shooting – what some of us might call real shooting, working spaniels through little rough woodlands and gorse, seeing woodcock in numbers unknown in the centre of England, meeting maybe a dozen species in a day. Local fishing is not to be sneezed at, either in the streams or at sea.

The broken country, full of steep little hills and deep valleys, looks as if God had laid it out for driving pheasants and partridges. Those lucky enough to live in the west are of the same opinion. Cornwall boasts some of the finest covert shooting in Britain. Take Caerhays Castle, for instance. A Gothic pile nestling amid woodlands and a famous rhododendron and magnolia garden a few hundred yards from the sea, in recent years it has become a Mecca for sportsmen. The Williams family, Caerhays's owners for 150 years, have lovingly fashioned drives to dream about, which test visiting guns to the limit. I turned up for a partridge outing which was billed as a 'small family day'. At the outset there were a lot of Orientally modest apologies for the humble nature of the fare: 'You really have to come for the pheasants in December to see this place at its best.' In the light of subsequent experiences, I want a fortnight at the shooting school before daring to do anything of the sort.

As we walked from the trailer to the first drive, a local fellow-gun filled me in on Caerhays: 'Think of it as Blandings Castle without the pig. But don't be fooled by the general air of chaos – they pretend to be tremendously laid back, but in fact it all works like clockwork. You never hear anyone need to raise his voice.' There were no pegs. Patrick Coombe, the former head keeper who now manages the Caerhays shoot and several others in the area, quietly placed the ten guns before joining the end of the line himself. The first partridges of the morning swung over the line, then disappeared into the next county almost unscathed.

I forgot to mention that there was half a gale blowing. Though some of the birds ducked under it, most came over the line like missiles, soaring and dipping on the wind, curling fiendishly. Some of us began to hit them only after increasing lead to about twenty feet. Shooting Caerhays-reared partridges seemed as thrilling as contending with grouse. Even with three or four good shots in the line, we were missing clouds of birds. 'The art of shooting flying is arrived at tolerable perfection,' *The Sportsman's Directory* observed smugly in 1792. I doubt whether its author had shot in Cornwall.

Every time the barrage died away and we waited for the horn, more birds came and still more, in a fashion a Spanish shoot would have been proud of. When we paused at last after maybe half an hour, most of us were emotionally exhausted. I wanted to turn the wind down 30 mph. Charlie Williams, who manages the five-thousand-acre estate, was gleeful about the flying lessons his pheasants were getting: 'By next month, after another day or two like this, they'll really know what's expected of them.' Caerhays can offer five different days on its own ground. At present the estate is shot fifty times a year, twelve of these by the family. Some guns down from the smoke rent shooting at two or three different local estates on successive days, to ring the changes. Julian Williams,

Charlie's father, says with pride: 'This isn't an "us-and-them" shoot – it's a "we" shoot.' The family is committed to preserving a sense of local community. There is a lot of laughter among guns, beaters, keepers – always a good sign at any sporting occasion. One of the guns, Alastair Sampson, has been coming to Caerhays for so long that he enjoys special privileges. At the outset Patrick said: 'This is a partridges-only day for everybody except Alastair, who can fire at anything because he will anyway.'

I killed a hen pheasant at the first drive because it was dead before it slowed down enough for me to see more than a brown blur. That was my story, anyway. It took a drive or two before I grasped the fact that Caerhays picking-up operates on the every-dog-for-himself principle. Once I got the message, as soon as I managed to hit anything I released my own beast to join an energetic race against a pack of local retrievers of every shape and size. The high wind – accompanied by rain after lunch – swiftly sorted us into sheep and goats. I was struggling, but four guns were shooting impressively by any standard: Patrick Coombe, Guy and Charlie Williams, and Max Kendry of the Game Conservancy. At one drive where I was standing beside a hedge, dead birds rained around me from an unseen gun on the far side, who turned out to be Max. I was suitably jealous.

Philip Tidball, a much-admired head keeper, has very young help: his under-keepers Jimmy Andrews and Leo Brown are aged nineteen and seventeen respectively – themselves both keepers' sons. These two teenagers were taking the strain for the first time that day, and there was much rejoicing at how well they did. Charlie Williams said: 'It's great to see them given the responsibility, and doing really well with it.' Although veteran keepers become beloved after many years on a place, it is striking to notice how many top-class shoots, especially grouse moors, are keepered by very young men. There are few jobs in which the demands on a man's energy and enthusiasm are so relentless.

I had never before shot in the far west. The exuberant mood of the day reminded me of my own old times living in Ireland. Like John Bull's other island, Cornwall is a wonderfully wild country, full of eager sportsmen who

cannot see why pleasures should be taken sadly. There is lots of shouting from almost everybody at almost everybody else. I am not sure I could indefinitely stand the weight of Cornish catering. One massive meal followed another, until after shooting we encountered the supreme temptation for any gun over twenty-five who will later have to eat dinner – tea in the castle on a scale to daunt a Soames. And the sport is as sparkling as Britain can offer.

It is often remarked that it is impossible to go shooting anywhere in Cornwall without meeting some member of the Williams tribe, who first colonised the county and its tin-mining industry a century and a half ago, and have been killing things there ever since. Fifty miles east of Caerhays, on a fine January morning I found myself contemplating a vista of brown bog and gorse, as a pack of wild dogs and even wilder guns advanced towards it. I enthused that it looked a perfect Irish scene. 'A perfect Cornish scene,' corrected Colonel Toots Williams emphatically. The Colonel was in no mood to be trifled with. A stiff shoulder had prevented him from achieving his customary annual bag of a hundred woodcock to his own gun. He was obliged to march unarmed. Come to that, he complains that nowadays he manages only forty-five shooting days a year. The Colonel is eighty years old, a cousin of Charlie Williams, and wholly delightful.

His son-in-law, the explorer, writer and conservationist Robin Hanbury-Tenison, explained to the assembled company, and to my acute embarrassment, that the day was being organised with the intention of driving snipe and woodcock in my direction. Fifteen guns grinned, though not as broadly as they did a few hours later when a couple of snipe went straight over my head unscathed. Robin was apologetic about the shortage of birds. 'It's just so wet,' he said. 'They're not in the bogs, they're all over Bodmin Moor.' At every drive, as a barrage greeted ten or fifteen snipe that rose, guns muttered that they had seen two or three hundred come off the place on a good day. Toots Williams, revered as one of the best woodcock shots in the country, said the trouble was that all the worms had burrowed six feet down to avoid drowning. Robin suggested that the first fruits of global warming in Cornwall looked like being a new breed of snipe with terribly long bills. I didn't mind about any of it. I was simply enjoying the sort of rough shooting that is almost extinct where I live, in the south of England. 'This is proper hunter-gatherer stuff,' said a gun as we plunged into a marsh behind a tribe of wet and happy dogs. 'The perfect place for spaniels.'

So indeed it is. Though Cornwall is proud of its driven shoots, the walked-up sport is what local guns boast about. They think nothing of driving sixty miles for a day chasing a few pheasants and snipe, just as I remember so many Irish shooters doing in the days when we lived in Kilkenny. 'Snipe-shooting is the second-easiest field sport to defend, after staghunting,' says Robin Hanbury-Tenison. 'We are preserving wetland habitat that would have vanished long ago if it wasn't for shooting. Farmers keep telling me they've got to drain this marsh or that one in case a cow falls in it. I ask them when they last remember a cow drowning in a bog, but it doesn't do any good. We can persuade them to protect the wetlands only because of sport.'

Robin has created a personal idyll based on the rambling farmhouse he shares with his wife Louella and a rotating cast of big children. They write and lecture, ride and do a bit of B&B, to make the most of the peerless views of Bodmin, looking out on their fifteen hundred acres of moorland. They are also building up a string of pretty cottages as holiday lets. If you call up a photograph of the seaside house on their website and don't like the mewing seagulls that go with it, the Hanbury-Tenisons invite you to click on the shotgun provided.

Though Robin is now well beyond sixty, his energy and enthusiasm are undimmed. He and the other guns plunged over fences and streams and through the rough spinneys with most of the puffing and panting coming from me. We were a noisy lot. Shouts, together with a lot of brrr-ing and tongue-clicking to stir the birds, echoed across the moor. Again and again, the silent flutter of a 'cock took me by surprise. The snipe may not have been there in the numbers those spoiled Cornishmen like, but there were enough to provoke repeated barrages. 'Have a go at anything – that's what we always say down here,' declared one gun cheerfully. As he strode briskly across the countryside, Toots Williams reminisced about shooting guinea fowl in Kenya in his days with the King's African Rifles. He lamented the difficulty of getting his former ninety days' shooting a year, 'unless one's able to get going in Scotland in August'.

The Hanbury-Tenison team drive their bogs perhaps three times a year, no more. Some are on Robin's land, while access to others depends on the goodwill of neighbours. Robin remarked that the great thing about a wet year was that even if it wasn't great for shooting, it was perfect for snipe breeding. The woodcock had come very late, everybody agreed, because it had been so mild in Scandinavia. We sloshed back to the Hanbury-Tenison compound in unfamiliar January sunshine for a hefty lunch, followed by a couple more drives. I was planted behind a solitary gorse bush, while two guns and their dogs walked a bog towards me and the others flanked it.

The snipe rose early in all directions, amid a lot of not very effectual banging, some of it from me.

We went home in the fading light with nineteen snipe, six woodcock and perfect contentment. Those Cornishmen are right: rough shooting is what the best of sport is all about. You walk far amid wonderfully wild countryside, work hard, hunt dogs and take your chance in finding game. How much I miss the chance to do more of this nearer to home.

23

Hitting Some Low Notes

To TELL THE truth about sport, one must be willing to include dog days as well as great ones, to notice failures which make the successes so rewarding. For instance, there was one summer morning when I gleefully told my son Harry that I was taking him on the sort of expedition which always produces action. The great thing about sea-fishing, I said, is that, unlike pursuing trout or salmon, you can be confident of finding something to catch. We were to take to the water off the Sussex coast with the Newhaven bass king, John Darling. John is dead now, but in his day was rather a famous sporting figure. At the prospect of going to sea with him, I felt confident of a failsafe outing. I was not even dismayed when John warned over the telephone that there was a small problem – no bass. A few seasons ago he landed two hundred, most of them monsters. That year, he had so far managed five. He suggested that we should go cod-fishing instead. Fine, I said.

Harry and I arrived at the quayside on a sunny August morning to find Darling looking like a bearded, weather-beaten Captain Hook before he lost his hand. This impressive pirate declared that we were going bass-fishing after all. The wind was whipping up in mid-Channel, where the cod were. We must stay inshore. Within minutes we were bouncing across the water at twenty-five knots on our way to catch the live bait Darling favours for bass. We reached a suitable wreck within long sight of Beachy Head, and threw out our mackerel lines. Filling the quota proved slow going. 'How many do we need for this?' I enquired. 'Oh, thirty or forty,' said Darling lazily. After ninety minutes and two changes of venue, we had landed fifteen. Harry began to look green as we wallowed in the swell. Couldn't we start after the bass with what we'd got, I asked. Why not, said John. He threaded up a couple of rods with floats, hooks and thirty-pound traces, laced a mackerel on each, ensured that it was swimming invitingly five or six feet below the surface, and began a long drift westward.

Then he stooped to scan the fishfinder screen. 'The trouble with this game,' he said, 'is that the fishing gets worse as the tackle gets better. The commercial boys find a shoal of bass and keep going back and going back, hammering the same spot until they've caught the lot. Last season they were making a real killing. This year, I doubt whether most of them are making any money at all.' Twenty years ago you could hardly give away a dead bass. But now that 'sea bass' stars on the menu of every self-respecting restaurant in Michelin, the price has soared to perhaps £4 a pound, nudging the quayside cost of lobsters. Pair-trawlers – two powerful boats towing a net between them – ply offshore between the rod fishers.

Every bass-catcher is watching the sea through binoculars from the cliff each day, looking to see who is doing what, where, and with how much success. If you think racing people tell each other shocking fibs about their horses, you ought to hear bass-fishers perjure themselves when they think they have identified a hot spot, and want to keep rivals out of range.

The young find lack of sporting success even harder to take than their fathers. Harry sat contemplating his immortal soul while we rolled past Peacehaven, a quarter-mile or so offshore. John photographed me reading a newspaper and smoking a cigar. We drank coffee and ate an expansive lunch, while our captain rolled his own horrible cigarettes and from time to time inspected the live-bait tank, round which the mackerel were lapping each other relentlessly. 'I was the first to get the idea of live-baiting bass out of Newhaven,' Darling said. 'Everybody thought I was barmy. But I've been fishing down here all my life, since the days when I started as a beach-caster. Nowadays everybody's using live bait. The fish can be incredibly spooky. You find a shoal, you have a couple of casts at them, and you find they've sugared off. But with GPS navigation, when you get the right drift and locate fish, you can precisely repeat the same course again and again.'

We hauled in our mackerel to make sure they were still cavorting convincingly, and watched the sea start to get up. 'I'm glad we weren't twelve miles out, looking for cod,' said John. 'We've got everything here, except the bass.' We felt for the poor man. It was all the editor of *The Field*'s fault, for telling me that Darling had only to

207

wave a hand and produce several loaves as well as any number of fishes. Our captain pointed out the spot where a mad-keen young bass-fisher from Farlow's spends every leisure hour casting from the end of an old sewage outlet. We scanned the movements of the gulls, which were stooping over what looked like mackerel shoals. John looked as if he might try to seduce us into going back to catch more mackerel. Forget the mackerel, we said.

Harry muttered that I had sold sea-fishing to him under a grossly false prospectus. John said that a hooked bass very seldom gets off. Harry demanded: 'In that case, where does the skill come in?' I said, 'It's just like stalking. The skill is with the boatman who finds you the fish, the way a stalker gets you up to deer. All the visiting angler needs to do then is to have himself photographed reeling them in.' At 3.30 p.m., I asked John for an honest assessment of our chances of catching a bass before nightfall. He chuckled: 'They're about the same as they've been every time I've been out this season.' I fancy, however, that this passionate fisherman still regarded us as a terrible pair of flakes when we pointed pleadingly towards the harbour entrance.

Next day, near home, I met a man who said that he had been out for bass three times in a month without touching a fin. As with all sporting activities, catching a fish would not be anything like the event it is if one hauled them out like – well, perhaps not mackerel – let us say whiting. 'Will you be able to write anything about bass-fishing if we haven't caught a bass?' Harry asked. Yes, I said. Readers get spoilt on writers' tales that always end in triumph. Every sportsman knows how many frustrations and disappointments intervene between each small success. I told the offspring: 'I shall write a truthful fisherman's tale, which ends with us driving home empty-handed. And, for once, we can be sure that every fisherman who reads it will believe me.'

Tweed on a Saturday, 5.15 p.m. Four other rods were packing up, sharing a farewell drink with the boatmen. I had a wife to collect from Berwick at 6.45, but for the past day or two the river had been growing lively towards evening. Net over my shoulder, I wandered up the path beyond the roaring falls, and picked a footing over the rocks beneath the sheer face. The Cauld pool of the Mertoun beat is a flat expanse of water checked by a rocky dam before the river pours steeply downhill towards the great pink road bridge. It fishes better a couple of feet lower than it stood on this October afternoon. But the bottom stretch was worth a try, and all of us had explored it with a fly over the previous couple of days.

A pair of herons watched sardonically as I began to roll cast into the unruffled current. With a heavy two-inch brass black-and-yellow tube, my amateur status as a roll caster felt secure. The fly was dropping into the water fifteen yards from the rod point, and I doubted this was far enough to reach the fish we had seen showing earlier. Behind me was a cliff of red stone. Between casts, I clambered clumsily over rocky debris at the water's edge.

It would be boring, possibly dangerous, to fall in here, with the torrent below. We had landed three fish off the beat that day, one of them caught by me – a stale eight- or nine-pounder. (No, I lie, the boatman insisted that it was a mere seven.) Since that excitement, however, I had touched nothing for a good many hours.

As always in these circumstances, I was growing melancholy. Was the fly too big? Would I ever learn to cast with the easy grace of my companions? After so many years when I thought myself a fortunate fisher, recent experience suggested that my lucky days were over. I gave up roll casting and tried flicking out line with a back cast along the cliff face. This worked better until I snagged the fly in a bush, mauling it severely as I tried to tug the line free. I cut away the remains and glanced at my watch: 5.25. I must be gone in twenty minutes. Was it worth tying on a new fly? Oh, why not? Once more, I began to cast. The line was curling round the boat moored just below me, a few feet short of the lip of the falls. It straightened. I tightened, and met immovable resistance. A snag? The resisting object at the other end of the line moved sluggishly, very sluggishly. It was a fish. My spirit soared, for I knew on the instant that it was a good one.

Rod point up, I felt a yard of line go, tightened the check on the reel, and glimpsed backing. The salmon was frighteningly close to the falls. I had to move it towards me, as far as possible from the leap. I applied a steady, heavy pressure. Very slowly, the fish began to swim upriver – five yards, ten, fifteen. Then it stopped. Once, twice, three times it jerked hard underwater. I hate headbangers. So often one loses them. I could feel the line singing metallically under tension, another sign I didn't much care for. I glanced at my watch again: 5.30. I began to worry about missing my wife at the station, and looked desperately downstream for a friendly face, for advice. I knew this was a big fish. I have caught my share of salmon, but have had less experience than I should like with heavyweights. The roar of the falls made shouting for assistance useless. For all my songs of my praise about the joys of fishing alone, this was a moment when I yearned for expert company.

The fish was boring downstream now, once more heading for the lip. Suddenly, it threw itself on its side out of the water. At least twenty pounds of fresh-run fish hung on the other end – still attached – as it splashed back into the current. I envisaged myself walking triumphantly into the hut, carrying that salmon by a nonchalant couple of fingers through the gills. What a way to end the week! What a wonderful return to luck! Once again, I began to move the fish slow and steady upriver. It was using every knot of the current to resist, edging off sideways, head three feet down.

I am never good at deciding how hard to fight fish. Over the years I have been taken to task by some gillies for being too gentle, by others for being too rough, and have lost salmon both ways. This time, the combination of the falls and the clock was making me impatient. I moved the fish upstream another ten yards. It now lay directly below my rod point. I had not dared to unsling the net from my shoulder. Grey of Falloden wrote many years ago: 'With a very large fish – the thought of losing which is really dreadful – I always have a secret fear of getting the net ready too soon, lest the act should be noticed by some unseen influence, and treated as a sign of that pride which deserves a fall.' I knew my salmon was nowhere near ready to come out, though we had been engaged almost fifteen minutes.

What next? It turned across the current, swimming steadily for the far bank. I let it go, the reel chattering beautifully. The line stopped. Once more I retrieved, leading the fish slowly back inshore. This could go on for hours. My shoulders were aching deliciously with strain and excitement. I thought: early this morning I was lying in bed wondering why I go on Scottish salmon-fishing, when one expends huge effort for slender reward. Now I was basking in all the million glorious reasons. There is no sensation, none on earth, to match the thrill of being connected to a great fish on one of the most beautiful rivers in Britain.

At last it was back within ten yards of my bank, holding stubbornly in the current. I recovered another yard of line. My watch said 5.40, and the fish must be good for another two or three runs yet. Thank God for big hooks and a strong anchorage. The fish stirred, drove for the surface and turned on its brilliant side five yards from my boots. The rod tip sprang straight, the fly ricocheted across the surface and clung to a rock a few feet up the path.

I retrieved numbly, gazing at the glossy surface of the pool, looking stupidly for the salmon. I walked back to the hut feeling as if I had climbed out of the wreckage of a car smash. My entrance broke up the conversation. 'I've just lost a big fish,' I announced. 'Bad luck,' they said, and started talking to each other again. How could they? Didn't they understand? This was a seminal moment in my life. I might never get over it. These heartless men didn't care. The boatman sounded as if he did not even believe it was a big fish. I wanted to sob.

As I drove like a dingbat for Berwick, however, I laughed at myself. I had been playing out the oldest fisherman's story on earth, the most unlikely to move any fellow angler, and least of all a doughty Tweed boatman. 'You would have landed it,' I told Mrs Hastings. 'You wouldn't have been in such a cursed hurry.' I awoke early next morning with no memory of the fish I had caught the day before. I was merely haunted by the snapshot of the one I had lost, throwing itself out of the water above the fall. Disappointments and failures etch themselves into the memory of every sportsman, while successes fade into mere scribbles in the gamebook.

24

Glorious Grouse

WELL, HERE WE are then. Butt six, second drive after lunch, on a breezy Yorkshire day when the grouse are skittish, Swaledale looks awesomely beautiful in late-afternoon sunshine with the shadows lengthening across the barns and neat green enclosures dotted below, and the beaters have the best part of two miles to come.

I am in seventh heaven. Sometimes I can take or leave driven pheasant-shooting, but there seems no pleasure more precious than shooting driven grouse. Pity all those hapless grandees who have been doing this all their lives, and who take it as much for granted as the breakfast egg.

Those of us who get into a butt a handful of times a year count those days as pearls in the necklace of sport, and thank our stars for every one of them.

The butt itself is a little masterpiece of dressed stone. I line up a dozen cartridges on its heather topping, plug in the ear defenders (two pairs atop each other, these days, in a belated attempt to defy mounting deafness), and lay the gun in front. My right-hand neighbour is straddled twenty yards back from his butt, watering away good claret into a patch of reeds. The gun on my left is already scanning the far distance – not an option for me, because my own horizon is only thirty yards ahead.

I like it that way. My best chance of hitting anything is to fire on instinct, rather than watch what is coming for half a mile. Odd, isn't it, that a covey seems to cross the moor so slowly for so long, then suddenly comes like smoke at the butt. Within a few seconds one is cursing oneself for leaving the birds too late. Most shooters become philosophers in grouse butts. In the midst of a busy life, suddenly you have half an hour and more before the birds arrive in which to contemplate God, nature, how much it must have cost to move the stone, who shoots with the Holland cartridges the decaying cases of which lie at one's feet, how they got the beaters up here in the days before motor vehicles, whether tweeds really keep you drier than Schoffels, and whether anyone would be terribly upset if, taking an away bird, a gun damaged one of the hikers marching blithely along the path behind the line.

Insofar as I possess any literary education, I have gained much of it waiting on moors for birds to come forward. There is no place like a grouse butt for reading huge tomes one has been meaning to address for years, while waiting for the first beater to show in the far distance. Dostoevsky, Stendhal, Gibbon – you name it, I've read it perched on a shooting stick in Yorkshire or Scotland. Some fellow guns and loaders regard this practice as eccentric, pretentious or downright unprofessional. I point out that for those of us who have trouble doing justice to the grouse when they start coming over, at least my method ensures that one ends up with some useful learning in the bag.

There is a sudden flurry of muffled reports on the right, and a big pack of grouse soars away to the rear, leaving a couple behind. September and October grouse look dramatically different from August ones. They are not merely bigger, they have abandoned the easy gliding of their summer youth. Instead of advancing towards the butts in a succession of reluctant short flights, with many never crossing the line at all, now they fly a mile and more without checking. Their urgent autumn wingbeat and jinking flight look different even in a still photograph. Bird crossing left. I have fired, dropped it and reloaded before even having time to think, which is the best way for me. Boom, on the right. Covey swinging straight over my butt. Bang, bang – too close. My neighbour shoots two behind. Another covey coming at me in front. Lead it, lead it – bang – one down in front – turn – fire again – it's down. I am euphoric. I get right-and-lefts at grouse sufficiently seldom to be allowed a silent cheer when it happens. Down the line, coveys are sailing across the contours, surging upwards as they cross the line, then whooshing past leaving a bird or two bouncing onto the heather. Damn. That lot have settled forty yards in front, and are standing, heads up, looking at us. Thirty seconds and they are off, back over the beaters, never to be seen again.

Why do we love grouse so much? Partly because they are fey and elusive, partly because grouse-shooting is a perpetual ambush which surprises us again and again, guns snatching shots at angles no driven pheasant- or partridge-shooter ever sees. A small covey coming left. I catch one and lose the second, then fail with both barrels at a long bird turning in front of the line. I love grouse on the wing with their soft feather and winking eye, and I love them even more passionately on the plate. I once went with a visiting house party to a Scottish dinner where the hostess greeted me with the unwelcome tidings: 'We were going to have grouse until we heard *you* were coming!' Oh God, what now? 'You once wrote about liking to eat two or three at a sitting. We didn't have enough for that, so we're giving you chicken instead.' Accusing looks from the rest of the team. Here was yet another house at which I scarcely dared show my face again.

Gunfire on the right – one bird down to my neighbour, a second going away just in shot, which I miss. Covey coming forward. I hit one and miss the second. Down the line, a steady procession of birds falling, as always, to a couple of deadly grouse shots who seem to do little else between August and December. Shut up, Hastings, jealousy will get you nowhere. But it is true that what distinguishes the men from the boys grouse-shooting is who can consistently take two from a covey rather than one.

The horn. The first beaters breast the ridge, flicking their flags noisily. Time to unload? Not quite. A single bird zips past, a yard above the deck. I touch it with a stray pellet which persuades it to settle reluctantly in the heather forty yards back, prey for a questing spaniel. Oh, the childish disappointment one feels when a grouse drive ends, the yearning for those coveys to keep coming and coming. It gets worse when the drive is the last of the day, when all that is left is to travel homeward remembering each bird one missed, and working out exactly what one should have done to kill it. I knew as I pressed the trigger that I was underneath that long grouse on the right when I was flank gun. I *must* learn to give them more lead behind. How could I have failed to drop even one from the fabulous covey which passed me ten feet out? Never mind. Like almost every grouse-shooting day, it was wonderful anyway.

25

Arctic Waters

$\mathscr{T}$HE MOST IMPORTANT change in the migratory cycle of British salmon fishermen over recent years is that many now go abroad in search of sport, after being so often disappointed in Scotland. Fishing in Russia, Alaska and Iceland is still a rich man's game, but so much money is hunting a diminishing number of salmon at home that distances scarcely seem to matter. I do not travel abroad as much as many fishermen, partly because I spent my formative years as a foreign correspondent. I have eaten camel dung, metaphorically anyway. I feel no urge to suffer in wild places. I want to be terribly comfortable. I once went to Alaska. It was an interesting experience, but one felt silly hauling in fish so easily. We became lazy about playing them. We knew that if we lost one, another would be along a couple of casts later. The most salmon that I have ever caught in a day outside Alaska was seven, on the Naver – four of these in rapid succession from the same pool. I packed up and went home happily, quite a while before the evening was spent. I felt that I had landed more than enough. To have continued hitting the shoal would have been meaningless.

Those who have not been to Iceland sometimes imagine that fishing there is pretty much like Alaska, with fish queuing to seize the fly. Yet few of my friends who fish the top Icelandic rivers catch more than an average of five or six per rod a day; riches by Scottish standards, but not overwhelming. Most Icelandic rivers produce more modest catches. You must work as hard for your fish as on a good Scottish river, but are likely to find water levels more reliable – though I have met Icelandic droughts, too. There are usually salmon to be caught, if you cast a respectable fly, but Icelandic fish are nothing like as suicidal as Alaskan ones. On my own last visit the British delegation which I joined was sharing one of the northern rivers with a group of Icelandic fanatics – what Alaskans would describe as 'meat fishers'. While we laboured to catch a fish a day at best (and I was not at best), the Icelanders bombarded the river with worms and baits to such effect that more than once they pulled half a dozen from a single pool in a morning. I have nothing against bait fishing, if that is what makes one happy. Worming is a skilled art. But it seems so boring playing a hooked fish on a bait rod that I prefer to labour in vain with a fly for the chance of playing a salmon on a sixteen-foot Sage.

Icelandic fishing gives new definitions to the colour of water. It is a cliché to talk of a river being gin-clear. Those cold green streams, flowing through miles of volcanic rock, possess a purity no peat stream can match. Almost everybody fishes a floating line. Our team was alternating between Scottish flies and big local horrors called Francises. As usual, there did not seem much difference in the results achieved. If one cast a decent line at a taking fish, one hooked it with any variety of fly. Presentation is always what matters, isn't it? In Iceland a couple of years ago I had my eye comprehensively wiped by Padraig Fallon, a formidable Irish fisher. I cast at a salmon in a canyon for a good hour one hot day, moving the fish a couple of times, changing flies constantly. Then I retired from the contest, and Padraig got to work. He cast beautifully. Second shot, that fish took, and was on the bank ten minutes later. I have discussed above the importance of luck to salmon-fishers. A skilled hand can do remarkable things, however, especially in low water.

Few countries convey as strong a sense as does Iceland of being a place where mankind clings to the edge of the earth. Even in July, amid the pale green grass and feast of wildflowers and birds, those infinite miles of lowering barren mountain threaten to close in and stifle the little red-roofed farmhouses perched precariously in their shadows. Utmost beauty derives from wisps of cloud hanging below the plateaux. Heaven knows how the Icelanders endure their winters, when endless night replaces the endless day of summer.

Because the fishing is so expensive, it is conducted in accordance with a relentless schedule. Most lodges get their rods to work at 7 a.m., fish until 1 p.m., lunch and sleep, then start again at 4 p.m. and fish until 10 p.m. The accommodation is austere. These are places merely to sleep and eat basic rations between assaults on the salmon. Wives lingering at home in Britain or America have little to fear about any spouse's misbehaviour on an Icelandic fishing trip. The bunks would defy a pair of midgets to achieve consummation. You can hear a pin drop from one room to the next, and anyway everybody is too tired for mere daylight bonking. It amuses me to see heavyweight British and American tycoons cohabiting in Icelandic lodges, in conditions that resemble those of Stalag Luft III circa 1943.

Except for the fishing, that is. Icelandic salmon are stunningly beautiful – fat, deep, their scales glistening like precious stones. In among the grilse, our party caught some fish in the high teens and early twenties which would make most Scottish fishers' mouths water. Leaving the wormers and bait fishers out of it, rods fishing flies in our party averaged a fish a day. Icelandic rivers vary a lot, but the ones I have seen achieve Tay or Spey dimensions in their lowest reaches, narrowing to Naver or Helmsdale size near the top. Weather in July and August, the only months that count, varies wildly. It can be as warm as a Scottish September, but more often feels windy and autumnal, even downright cold. It can also be very, very wet. On the credit side, however, there is seldom significant midge or mosquito trouble.

In a country of only 270,000 people where salmon fishing is a major source of income, in the happiest way you feel that every local is on your side, pleased for you to be there, keen for you to catch fish, in a way that is sadly less assured in modern Scotland. Also, of course, Icelandic government policy supports rod fishing and conservation in a manner unthinkable in Britain, or at least unthought by any British government as urban as those of recent times. I have never hit a real winning streak in Iceland –

on four trips either the weather has been wrong, fish have been short, or I have just not cast well enough. But friends have caught some wonderful fish, and come home euphoric. This is class fishing, in a way that Alaska is not. I am teasing a bit about the austerity of Icelandic lodges – every basic amenity is there.

Any fisherman who tires of slim pickings in Scotland and is lucky enough to get an invitation or even an opportunity to write a cheque for a trip to Iceland should get on his bike to Reykjavik. It costs an arm and both legs, but it is a joy for any fisher who loves the feel of strong, cold currents racing past his waders, and the chance of a glittering silver fish on the end of the cast.

There is a delightful passage in Trollope's novel *The Duke's Children*, where young Lord Silverbridge arrives on a Perthshire moor and declares it 'infernally ugly'. His host, a big shot named Reginald Dobbes, answers contemptuously: 'If you come after grouse, you must come to what the grouse think pretty.' This exchange sprang to mind as I gazed for the first time on the legendary Varzuga, at the heart of the Kola peninsula. It is jolly lucky salmon think the river pretty, because nobody else could. An endless flat vista of tundra and stunted conifers reaches to the horizon. In the last days of May the Varzuga, about the size of the Thames at Chelsea, is one of the few things in Russia which looks as if it is hurrying.

We scurried to assemble our rods. It had taken twenty-seven hours to reach this fisherman's shrine from Gatwick, and we wanted to make up for lost time. Eager to ensure that we got an adventure holiday, air traffic control at Murmansk whimsically refused landing clearance to the regular Roxtons' charter plane which was carrying us. Indeed, after two hours circling the airport pleading with the authorities, our pilot reported that the Russians had told him that unless we left their air space, they would send up fighters to escort us on our way. One might call this the spirit of Stalingrad.

We landed at a Finnish airport named Ivalo, which made Rockall seem a teeming metropolis. Young Charlie White from Roxtons, who would have done well at Dunkirk, organised a hasty lunch for sixty and then a coach, which whisked us to Murmansk in eight hours, three of them spent at Russian border control. Nobody had informed its stony-faced officers that the Cold War is over; or maybe our interminable processing was just their revenge for losing it. About now you will be ready to hijack the Washingtonian's line on the morning of 15 April 1865: 'But apart from that, Mrs Lincoln, how was the play?' How was the fishing? Pretty good, actually. I would urge a novice not to make his first cast in Russia, because there is usually a wind, and a good many places where it is tricky to get a fly out unless one is a competent Speycaster. Early in the season, however, most fish lie under the bank. The highest scorers on our beats proved to be two Frenchmen who, we learned when we met up at the end of the week, had cast relentlessly fast and short. Our own team tried to throw longer lines. We hooked plenty of fish, but with hindsight wasted a lot of time and energy getting the fly to them.

I made an early nonsense. At the Kola, one can use only barbless double hooks. I simply cut a barb off a treble, and lost close to twenty fish before I realised something was wrong, got some proper doubles, and parted with very few salmon thereafter. Although the Brits have given all the Varzuga fishing places names as 'pools', in truth at that height of water one is simply casting into a featureless expanse, relying on the Russian guides to point out hot spots. On our first afternoon I landed eight grilse, more than I have netted in a day in Scotland for twenty years. Most of our team were doing likewise. We boated home to a delicious dinner in the camp – the food and comfort of the cabins were among the best surprises of the week – then went to bed except for a couple of fanatics who picked up their rods again.

It was the same through the days that followed. There were still patches of snow on the ground. Waddling down to the boats in all those layers of kit and a lifejacket, one felt more like a Tornado pilot than a fisherman. But modern clothing is so good that we never felt cold. Some of us had hoped to do some fishing with single-handed rods, but in those conditions it never seemed a starter. We saw an osprey, lots of terns, white hares, eagles. Conversation with the gillies was monosyllabic, reflecting our lack of Russian and theirs of English, and often very funny.

'Coffee?' Sergei asked my partner and me one morning.

'Oh yes, please,' we said eagerly.

He searched in his bag and shrugged: 'Sorry, no coffee,' which is a fable of modern Russia.

As he unhooked a fish, I would say hopefully: 'Four kilos?'

Decisive headshake: 'Three and half, maybe.'

My fishing mate asked Sergei how he likes modern Russia. 'Communism better,' he answered, as do so many of his compatriots.

After three days on the lower Varzuga, the helicopters flew us a few miles to the Kitsa, a tributary about Tay size with much more character in its upper reaches. There were runs and eddies where we had some wonderful tussles with those strong, brilliant fish. On our last two days, the sun came out. I watched the bright light shimmer on companions' rods far down the bank as they bent over salmon, and listened to a host of noisy cuckoos as our own flies drifted across the torrent. The lower Kitsa holds lots of fish, but is pretty dreary water, flanked by dense willow bushes to catch a hook. It also proved heavily populated with Russian fishers who monopolised some of the best places, apparently by consent of the local warlord who controls everything in that part of the world. Nobody ventured to argue the toss with the Russian casters, though I thought it was a bit thick when one of them, anchored stubbornly downstream of me, borrowed our gillie, Viktor, to photograph himself with a fish. But then, Viktor himself liked to wield a spinning rod between us when he was not netting salmon. The Kola is pretty much the Wild West, where anything goes.

Maybe two thousand British anglers now go to Russia annually. Most of them come home very happy, and return year after year. We had been warned not to expect many big fish so early in the season, and indeed the biggest

I caught was eight pounds – I never saw my backing all week. The largest salmon caught by our party was around ten pounds. Our top scorer (the Frenchmen were in the team that swapped beats with us midweek) caught forty-four, our unluckiest performer had seventeen, and I landed thirty-four. I give those figures simply as clues to what one might expect at that time in that place. If we had been 'trophy fishers', as some Kola anglers are, determined to hammer the water every hour God makes in order to pile up numbers, we could have had more. Our group, however, preferred to enjoy the comforts of the camps between sorties. The English staff could not have been more helpful, charming or efficient. My only gripe was that it would have been a help to be able to call on expert advice from someone who really knew the water – the gillies are simply net-wielders and boatmen.

One of the joys of fishing in Scotland is that, even if one is not catching salmon, the setting is incomparable. Most people would only find the Kola lovely if they were on day-release from Belmarsh nick. But it is one of the world's great wildernesses, which possesses a majesty of its own, and harbours salmon in numbers few British fishermen have seen at home for decades. To fish the Kola is a remarkable experience. We travelled home un-eventfully, leaving some passengers with a faint sense of anticlimax that the Russians had deprived us of an opportunity to tango in mid-air with their MiGs.

26

Nightlife

$\mathscr{B}$ECAUSE OF THE odd hours I work, I get to see more dawns than most people. I was reflecting testily the other day that there is little joy in first light perceived from a car or through plate glass. What a thrill it is, however, to meet the same spectacle out of doors, in wild places; to see darkness ebb away on a hill, riverbank or in a cornfield; to perceive shapes sharpening, shadows becoming living creatures and dim masses turning into woods and hill faces. Full daylight is almost an anticlimax after the long, mysterious minutes which precede it, above all in Africa.

228

No one who cares about the countryside can claim to know much about it until they have grown familiar with its sensations during the hours when urban humanity is sitting indoors amid bright lights. Man is one of the few mammals at a loss in darkness. Much of the natural world is, of course, far livelier while humans are asleep. It is either hunting, or in peril of being hunted. If we want to reach out to nature, or at least to many of the most fascinating parts of it, we must do so by learning to walk and watch in the darkness. Thus the magic of sea-trout fishing on July nights, of lamping foxes or rabbits, of watching badgers and owls.

One among many reasons that I enjoyed the years which I spent among armies in my younger days is that, like foxes and badgers, battlefield soldiers are most active during the dark hours. I have shared some wonderful experiences with warriors at times when the rest of the world has been asleep. I once interviewed a former German Panzer officer, who told me that he found fighting the Americans during the Second World War a far less disagreeable experience than confronting the Red Army, because the 'Amis' left them alone at night: 'I think the Americans liked their sleep just a little bit too much,' he declared mischievously. For centuries, the art of the soldier embraced many of the skills of the hunter and his quarry, above all during the hours of darkness, when he who was most sensitive to his environment was most likely to come home alive.

At one time and another I have spent a lot of hours trudging across Welsh mountains and Scottish glens in the blackness, and usually also amid rain. In the countryside, nothing does more for one's confidence than to overcome by experience the natural fear of the dark that most of us start with. Many grown-ups are prone to an instinctive sense of unease in woodland at night, until familiarity relaxes us. It is a reflection of the hazards of modern urban life that my wife declares that she feels no tremor of unease walking our dogs at midnight in the fields behind our house, while she is deeply uncomfortable doing the same thing in Fulham.

For a gamekeeper, of course, to work at night, to sharpen his senses and above all his hearing, is second nature. The rest of us, even if we cannot match the professionals, can learn to move in the sunless hours more easily than we expect, and to see more than we think possible in a darkness that is seldom absolute. Among the curses of the modern countryside are the distant glowing lakes of light overhanging our towns and villages, almost inescapable save in the remoteness of Wales and Scotland. Libby Purves has written well about the curse of 'light pollution', the belief that it is proper and natural to bathe the most rustic hamlet in a sodium glare. Most modern villagers now seem to want illumination. Yet, properly to experience the countryside at night, our eyes should not have to compete with unnatural light, even in the distance. We should be focusing every sense to detect hints of animal movement.

Woodland stalkers and wildfowlers become expert at exploiting the last leavings of light in a fading sky. Even an amateur duck-shooter like myself loves those moments of straining to catch the hint of a dropping teal, firing at a flash of movement and blinking in the red flare of one's own muzzle-blast.

Despite my remarks above about animals being in their element in darkness, I once had an old dog who wouldn't touch a duck once night fell. As long as light persisted, she would dive in after anything. But when darkness came, some obscure canine trade union compelled her to down paws. It was irksome to have to wade about by torchlight doing her job, while she sat impassive by the lakeside, waiting to go home.

More and more countrymen, including keepers, now regard a night-vision sight as a normal fashion accessory. This is cheating, of course. I have borrowed night-vision kit from time to time. I found it wonderful in twilight, much less effective in deep darkness. But if technology continues to advance apace, in a generation we shall find that even keepers and poachers have exchanged a vital part of their finely-tuned natural instincts for a battery of electronic equipment from Dixon's.

Africa is the most exciting place on earth to explore in darkness, though only a fool would do so without expert guidance. The sights and sounds of night in the bush are irresistibly dramatic and vivid. A sense of danger, spurious or otherwise, sharpens every moment. And after the long hours of cold and night comes the peerless experience of an African dawn: the great red light, the muffled murmur of sleepy voices, the scent of woodsmoke, the first rays of warmth spreading across the bush. I have most often experienced African nights when reporting wars. If an element of risk from human malevolence is overlaid on the odours and tensions created by nature and wild beasts, every sense is alert every moment.

There was also a time when I rented a Scottish place

where I could go stalking alone at first light. How I loved to do this. On one of those magical mornings I came round a crag to find myself six feet from a perching eagle, the sort of reward one earns by setting off hiking at 5 a.m. Likewise, I believe that the young should discover what it is like to walk in darkness and rain, to camp and cook in the wilderness, to dress and pack and march with a burden before dawn, even if they intend to spend all their later lives in comfort and cities.

My belief in the value of early training outdoors, and amid inhospitable conditions, stems not from seeking to condition my offspring or anybody else's to become soldiers, but from wanting them to feel a self-confidence about traversing the wild places in darkness as well as daylight. Assurance in oneself grows in a remarkable fashion when one discovers that the body can overcome discomfort and exhaustion, cold and wet. He who knows the countryside only in sunshine and daylight knows it hardly at all. Does that sound terribly old-fashioned and Buchanesque? I hope so.

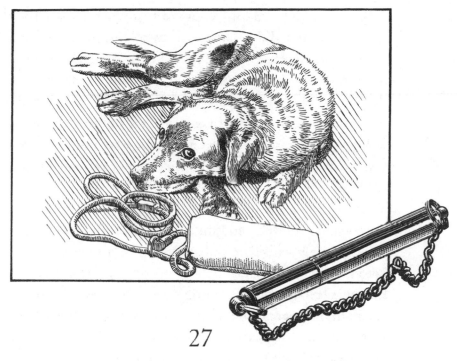

27

Saying Please and Thank You

In a Yorkshire lodge last season, I was captivated by a cushion embroidered with the wry observation: 'You never realise how many friends you've got until you buy a grouse moor.' Now, to shooting folk this is a truth about life as important as Archimedes' first principle, or Dorothy Parker's observation on the fate of girls who wear glasses. Men who own grouse moors lie awake at night agonising about whether anybody loves them for themselves, or whether their own wives are being nice only to soften them up to provide invitations for their lovers. It is not dukes and earls who inspire a Red Sea parting of respectful worshippers at rural social occasions these days, it is moor owners. It is an embarrassing truth that while in America a newly rich tycoon can achieve social status most readily by good works, especially giving millions to arts institutions, in Britain purchasing a moor is a much faster track to deference, if not respectability.

Grouse-shooting is the most thrilling of all sports. There is not a lot of it about. To afford to pay £120 a brace to rent driven shooting, you need to be almost rich enough to buy a moor outright. Thus, almost all of us who get the odd chance at driven grouse depend on the kindness of friends. The sound of sobbing, with gratitude or disappointment, is heard up and down shooting Britain when the postman delivers at invitation time. It is all very well for you to mutter something about passing the sick-bag, but this is true, isn't it? In some degree, the same tensions prevail about all manner of sporting invitations, unless one lives in one of those corners of wildest Britain where everybody shoots or fishes all the time because there is nothing else to do but sexually harass sheep.

People ask each other to shoot for one of four reasons: to entertain relations or friends; in pursuit of commercial advantage; in the expectation of being invited back; or because the guest is an uncommonly good shot. I am not sure that even the last virtue counts for as much as once it did. A popular friend of mine, who shoots very straight and lives amid a cluster of grouse moors, tells me that he gets fewer days than he used to, because almost every spare gun is let.

One consequence of the irresistible pressure to rent shooting is that in bumper years nothing like enough birds get killed, because many of the tenants simply do not shoot well enough, especially later in the season. In former times, in November and December moor-owners invited every crack shot in the area, regardless of social graces, simply to get the grouse killed. Nowadays, many paying guns lack the skill and experience to deal effectively with back-end grouse – and here I do know what I am writing about.

Seriously big shots suffer agonies about juggling invitations, the anguish of accepting in April a date for a modest day's partridges in Hampshire, only to find that in June they are offered a grand outing in Yorkshire for the same day. Even those of us with more modest sporting programmes suffer the occasional clash. I have committed almost every social *faux-pas* in the book, but I respect nanny's advice about never switching horses, trading upmarket. One gets found out. A sporting guest of my acquaintance, whom we shall call Rembrandt, is notorious for the ruthlessness with which he manages his diary, as was once demonstrated by experiment. A mischievous friend wrote asking him to a modest south of England pheasant day. This invitation was promptly accepted. The writer then forged a letter from some grandee inviting this Rembrandt to a blue-chip shoot in Yorkshire for the same date. The fish rose unerringly to the fly, and wrote to his first host explaining that unavoidable commitments made it impossible to attend, and so on. He took a lot of teasing over that one, but is beyond shame about these matters.

Surtees observed that country social life operates on the

debtor and creditor principle. We must acknowledge the truth of this. People who own great shoots do not expect their guests to respond with invitations on the same scale, but it is hardly surprising that the people who get most shooting are those best placed to ask their hosts back. I like the remark of the rough-hewn tycoon who growled: 'When I've had 'em shooting twice, I want to be asked for a cuppa tea. I don't want the tea – but I wanna be asked!'

A wartime Guards ensign tells my favourite invitation story. He spent the icy, dreary winter of 1939 at Windsor Barracks. There was nothing to do, no one to fight, not much to eat or drink. The regiment paraded and shivered in attendance on the monarch. Just before Christmas, however, there was a small interruption of the tedium. A certain Captain Arthur James found himself walking on air around the mess for several days. He had been invited by his King to shoot in the Great Park. On the night before the great event, however, the telephone rang. The Mess Corporal called out for Captain James. It was the King's equerry, speaking in the funereal tones reserved for deaths and abdications: '*You never told us you were divorced.*' Captain James enquired in bewilderment what on earth that had to do with anything. The equerry demurred: '*You don't suppose that you can shoot with King George VI if you are divorced?*' The hapless officer exploded. 'I see how it is,' he wailed in anguish. 'I'm good enough to shoot the King's bloody enemies, but I'm not good enough to shoot his bloody pheasants!'

Those of us who receive invitations neither for our shooting prowess nor because we own shoots are expected at least to keep our end up in other respects. A decade or two ago I was invited for a shooting weekend. A few days beforehand, there was a heavy scene at home about parental duties. I rang my host and explained that though we couldn't make the weekend, I would still love to come and shoot. Rising early on the day, I drove a hundred

miles across England and mustered with the guns. My host's wife strolled out of the house. 'Morning, Max,' she said sweetly. 'What I always say is: "If you want to shoot, join a syndicate." We're not so desperate for people to kill our pheasants that we have to bus them in. *When we ask you for a weekend, we want you for a weekend!*' I reeled before the onslaught and hardly touched a feather all day. She was right, of course. I hope I learned the lesson. Even if a guest can't masquerade as Lord Walsingham on the peg, the least he can do is sing for his supper afterwards.

The hardest part of sport starts when it is all over, and the time comes to express gratitude. 'Thank you for the birds that sing,' goes the hymn, 'thank you Lord for everything.' The Church of England is riven by schisms these days, but I fear the clergy would close ranks against adding a couple of lines of the kind every sportsman sings in his heart: 'Thank you for the birds we shoot, thank you Lord for last week's spate.' That may not rhyme, but you know what I mean.

We can murmur private appreciation on our knees in church for most of the good things that come our way, but offering earthly thanks to those who invite us to shoot and fish presents a knottier problem. A young gun asked my opinion the other day about the necessary length of the letter to our host after two days' grouse-shooting. 'Would four sides do, do you think?' he enquired hopefully. I answered cautiously that it depends how big his handwriting is. Since I have composed all my life on a keyboard, thank-you letters represent my only efforts at penmanship. The outcome causes many recipients to demand crossly how I make a living without having learned to write legibly. I can offer no excuses. I try my best, but somehow only a hieroglyphic jumble emerges. John Keegan, also a professional scribe, is the only man I know whose handwriting is worse than mine. There are moments when I fancy that even punctilious hostesses would be grateful if both of us abandoned our manual efforts, and addressed them legibly by e-mail.

A mean-spirited sporting host would file everybody's thank-you letters from year to year for comparison. Those who use exactly the same wording every season would be exposed to derision, even if they protested feebly that Eton or Harrow or wherever did not encourage original thinking. I know of only one guest who habitually tells the truth in his post-*battue* correspondence. As Saki vividly explained, such a social policy is disastrous. My chap considers himself an arbiter of sporting matters, and could have won Olympic medals for boorishness. Thus, he has frequently informed a host that: a) he did the third drive the wrong way around; b) the beating line made a ridiculous amount of noise; and c) people shouldn't waste other people's time by making them turn out for a day on which the bag fell below three hundred. Unsurprisingly, this correspondent nowadays has to pay for his sport everywhere except on the estates of a couple of flagellants who think him comic.

Most of us go to the opposite extreme, declaring fulsomely that the day was so wonderful we didn't mind the snowstorm a bit. If we have fished for a blank week, we say that the pleasure of watching the oystercatchers on the riverbank made it all seem worthwhile. If we drew a peg next to our worst enemy, we avow that the occasion gave us a chance to see the man in a completely new light, without adding that we realised he is a cad as well as a bounder.

On odd occasions when I am on the receiving end of thank-you letters, I am fascinated to observe how many writers are fans of the old *Down With Skool* books. That is to say, they draw heavily upon the Molesworth all-purpose circular: 'Dear Aunt/Uncle/Pater, thank you for the space gun/rocket ship/chocolate cake. It was wizard/stale/broken already.' Just as Little Red Riding Hood was much impressed by what big eyes the Wolf had, so it is astonishing what big writing some correspondents develop when

239

trying to make it to a second page without mentioning the weather.

Jokes apart, thanking people for sport poses a notable problem. If one is asked to a dinner party, beyond the pain of being expected to listen to one's conversation, the cost to a host is not very great. But anybody invited to a day's shooting or fishing, never mind several days', is given a pearl of huge price, even if some expression of gratitude should go direct to a company's shareholders. Most people who go grouse-shooting, me included, could not do so if we were obliged to pay the commercial going rate. We are dependent on the generosity of others. Finding the right words to express gratitude without becoming a cringing sycophant would strain the pen of Milton, though I am uncertain how much time he himself spent in the butts. Matters become especially tricky if something ghastly happened during one's stay. It is debatable whether writing 'Such a disappointment for poor Johnny to be off form at the second drive before he popped his clogs during the third' strikes the right note. In the event of anything other than a fatality, it is probably safest to pretend that one never noticed anything amiss, though flashing blue lights can be conspicuous on the hill.

There was an old, grand, social convention that one should never mention food or drink in a thank-you letter, on the grounds that to do so implied that one expected these to be less than perfect. This was silly a hundred years ago, and is even sillier now. When a hostess has taken a lot of trouble to arrange the browsing and sluicing, it is pretty rude not to mention how thrilled were the guests by the outcome. If a host produces magnificent wine, there is not much chance he will ever do so again, if the company treats Haut-Brion as carelessly as Waitrose infuriator.

One friend of mine every year urges a mutual non-aggression pact, or rather an agreement that neither of us will write to the other to thank him for hospitality received. He thinks I have an unfair advantage, because I write for a living and can therefore presumably compose a mere letter in three minutes. Not so, not so. The sporting thank-you letter makes writing books seem a doddle.

Navigating a course between the perfunctory Moles-worthspeak circular and the wildly extravagant happiest-day-of-my-life-since-our-chief-executive-fell-under-a-bus is a challenge for titans. Missing the damn birds is the easy part. It is what comes afterwards that tests a sportsman to the limits.

28
Level Pegging

$\mathscr{I}$ HAD A poor draw last Saturday – out of the shooting all day, chafing on my number as birds streamed over neighbours on both sides. But the Saturday before, Five proved a magic number for me. I know I fired more cartridges than anybody else in the line. That is the charm of drawing for places at driven shoots. It is pot luck who gets the best of the game. Over a season, good pegs and bad ones even out. Mind you, when one is standing doing nothing in a heavy drizzle, while down below one can hear a barrage of gunfire, none of the above sweet reason offers protection against ignoble jealousy.

Unless you know a shoot very well in all weathers, you never can tell which numbers on a given day are likely to put you in the money. I was Nine on the edge of a Gloucestershire wood at the end of a thin day recently. I tramped through the mud to my appointed rendezvous without extravagant hopes. But as the beaters tapped forward, almost every bird in the spinney scuttled magnetic-

242

ally towards my corner, then took off and flew back in succession over the trees until I had emptied a belt of cartridges. I went home with my tail wagging as happily as my dog's.

I wish more shoots would put the end man in the line behind the beaters. Standing out in front, again and again one sees marvellous birds turn and soar away to the rear, especially if there is a treeline for them to follow, and even more so if there is a wind. An idea persists in some circles that it is *infra dig* to ask somebody to be a back gun. I will take the job any time. It is also a joy to be given a roving commission behind the line. All right, one dances around a lot in pursuit of the last flush of pheasants rather than hitting the right spot for the next one, but often one gets chances at really sporting birds others have missed. For us duffers, there is the added pleasure that the line can't see what we are doing.

Some of the judgements about how a line is placed depend on how many birds a host wants to shoot. Very few pheasant or partridge drives in Britain can comfortably accommodate eight or nine active guns in a straight line – one or two are always likely to be spectating. Often an owner knows that the heaviest weight will fly over, say, Four, Five and Six. If he wants to get the bag up he will double-bank, with two or three high numbers deployed behind. If not, then not.

A few years ago I was a guest at a pretty horrible commercial shoot in Wiltshire, where the bag looked thin by lunchtime. Afterwards, we found ourselves placed fifteen yards apart in a double line. Birds were then funnelled overhead, crossing the guns within a fifty-yard front, like aircraft at an interminable fly-past, scarcely one a challenging target. They kept coming for half an hour. A lot were shot – so many that our host had a row about the bill with the owner afterwards. I suggested asking this notoriously hard-boiled egg why the drive was not stopped when the score became absurd. 'I've never stopped a drive in my life,' said the owner defiantly. Some grudging compromise was eventually achieved, but this was plainly not a shoot to visit twice.

A wind, of course, can change everything. Suddenly One and Two or Eight and Nine become hot spots; the middle guns can find themselves spectating while pheasants stream over the most unlikely pegs. How we all yearn for wind. Every shoot becomes vastly more exciting, as long as it is possible to shift the guns to meet the conditions. At very high shoots I am sometimes grateful to be placed rather than to draw, simply because thoughtful hosts stick me where I might be able to hit something occasionally, rather than on the pegs where the superbirds will fly. I am thinking of one Yorkshire escarpment in particular, which produces magnificent pheasants. The height of the birds varies, more or less predictably, with the steepest on the right and the (marginally) less alarming on the left. I stood on the right once, and found myself completely outclassed. These days, my host knows my form well enough to put me on the port side. I am not offended. I know my limitations. I can tackle some of those birds swinging wide on the open flank. I am merely wasting lead trying to hit the cabin-pressure pheasants 140 feet or so above my right-hand neighbours.

At some shoots, the host makes Byzantine arrangements for even-numbered guns between drives to take one pace to the rear, while odd numbers are told to shut their eyes and count to twenty. With the good old system of moving up two, one has the same neighbours all day, which is nice; and somehow everybody gets a turn. With evens-up-odds-down, one can find oneself on the edges three or four times in a day. And nobody but the host understands the whole nonsense anyway.

At a few socially ambitious shoots there is no problem about remembering numbers, because the owner operates a straightforward caste system. Prominent guests are invited to stand in the middle at every drive, while other ranks get plonked wherever is left. This is not flattering. One day in Gloucestershire, a distant Royal connection and a couple of aristocratic Germans were given the centre pegs at every drive. I found myself outside gun three times, took the hint, and have not been back, even for a chance of potting one of the junkers.

It is much easier to be phlegmatic about the placing of guns or the luck of the draw if one gets a lot of shooting. You know that if you miss out today, better things could happen next week. When I was younger, however, and only got four or five driven outings a year, a thin day invited sobbing all the way home. It was all so unfair. Why was it that even pheasants were given to him that hath? Nowadays, I have nothing rational to complain about. Except . . . Well, er, now you come to mention it, Seven was kept miserably out of it last week. Don't you agree?

29

New Ways and Old

*A*NEIGHBOUR WHO loads on several local estates asked me the other day, 'Do you see a lot of people not picking up what they shoot, nor tipping the keeper?' Not many, I said, but maybe I'm lucky. He went on to detail some of the shooting parties he had attended lately, almost all corporate, where these little details were omitted. In fairness, he added, some of the guns had never shot before. One team arrived with accompanying instructors from a shooting school.

Stories like this provoke mixed feelings. Apologists would argue that the more people who practise field sports, the better. The bigger business shooting becomes, the better it can make the case for its own importance when opponents turn their attentions to getting it banned, as they surely will. Yet I am sceptical about whether financial arguments carry any weight at all with Parliament, or with the public. Although the sums of money spent on field sports seem large to us, they remain tiny in terms of the economy as a whole. Likewise, and as with fox-hunting, the fact that a million people shoot is only a modest deterrent against political action by New Labour, because it calculates that most of those million vote Tory anyway.

The case for shooting will be decided chiefly by environmental arguments. In presenting these, the manner in which we shoot seems very important; hence the unease about big bags and the insensitivity towards the countryside sometimes displayed by novices. To say this is not sporting Nimbyism, an attempt to keep others from sharing our pleasures. On the contrary, we should do everything possible to help the young get going, and to encourage urban-dwellers to share traditional pastimes. I am simply reflecting upon an inescapable soullessness about the experience of shooting where a team of guns arrives at a given location, hitherto unknown to them, stands beneath successive clouds of birds for a few hours without human contact with those presenting them, then disappears into the night, never to be seen again.

At some commercial shoots, guns feel themselves being processed rather than entertained. My own periodic skirmishes with pickers-up are inspired by the fact that at such places guns seldom bring their own dogs, and are resented when they do. One day last season, after a drive at which everything behind me was picked up before the final horn went, I was working my Labrador towards one of the only three birds left in front. A picker-up's spaniel snatched it. 'Sorry, sir,' said its owner triumphantly. 'No, you're not,' I said crossly.

The point about this story is that regulars at the shoot regarded visiting guns as mere birds of passage, indeed almost interlopers. The occasion belonged to them far more than to us. We were spending a day on a production line, then disappearing forever from their lives, to be replaced by another faceless gaggle of customers three days later. I sulked furiously about the pickers-up, though they had the last laugh when I forgot to put my own dog in the car after the last drive, and had to slink sheepishly back ten minutes later to retrieve him. I drove home brooding about what we can do to maintain the spirit of traditional shooting, in an age when it is in danger of losing its heart by selling itself on the open market, by becoming an industry rather than a communal activity.

For a start, more could be done at the start of a day to introduce guns to the 'home team'. Often, a head keeper is away with the beaters and is not encountered at all until met for a tip after the last drive. It is now deemed necessary for legal reasons to conduct Health & Safety briefings. First-time visitors would benefit from also being told a little about a shoot and who makes it tick, and about how the drives are being done. It may be argued that this would 'waste' ten minutes of a short winter's day, yet it seems worthwhile to make us more involved in a place than as a mere paying marksman – or, in my case last season, missman. Novices should be told that it is appropriate to pick up the birds around one's peg, and that a gesture of recognition to the keeper at the end of the day will be appreciated. Some corporate hosts assure guns that they will 'take care of the keeper'. This seems mistaken generosity, because it further depersonalises the whole experience.

It is not a bad test of anything we do to imagine how it would look if it was being televised. An informal group of men, women and dogs walking fields and hedges in pursuit of game –rough shooting – is bound to seem more sympathetic than any driven day. If such an occasion as the latter is conducted as if it were a winter version of the company box at Ascot, with champagne at elevenses and Lynch Bages for lunch, then to any outsider it can start to look creepy, if not outright vulgar. We base our claims for shooting on the argument that it is a traditional country sport. To make this stick, surely there should be some attempt by all those involved to engage with the countryside, rather than merely to move a boardroom from the Square Mile to a patch of Hampshire or Suffolk.

Some readers may suggest that my attitude represents inverted snobbery, or maybe hypocrisy, since I have taken part in more than a few Citified days myself. In the times in which we now live, however, it seems essential to ask ourselves questions about the way we do things, if we want them to continue. In the twenty-first century, field sports will be under relentless scrutiny and criticism. If a corporate culture is allowed to dominate what was once a low-key rural pastime, then the image of shooting will seem wholly unsympathetic. If our sport becomes perceived merely as a company paintballing outing with vast numbers of live creatures for targets, I would not bet on its surviving to 2100, and it will not deserve to.

It seems essential to seek to keep alive the old ideal of sport, which focuses not on formal social gatherings at which birds are hired to provide a cabaret, but instead on the traditional vision of hunting for a quarry. Towards the end of the morning at a shoot in Suffolk last season, a fellow guest leapt with sprightly enthusiasm towards a terrier and a cluster of excavations beside a gatepost. 'Right!' he cried. 'Last drive before lunch! Ratting!' There was an inconclusive scurry of dogs around all those delicious scents, our gun urging them on with every symptom of preparing to dive down a hole himself. I thought: Here we have the compleat sportsman. This bloke is significantly north of fifty years old, yet he has the instincts of a poacher and the eagerness of a teenager. I have seen him hanging over a hopeless stretch of tangled foliage above a river bank, questing for an opening to cast for the fat, smug sea trout which lay secure beneath. He will chase a duck, a pheasant, a salmon, a grouse in any conditions, and maybe by any means. He shoots straighter drunk than I do sober, and casts a line to die for. He is one of life's natural hunter-gatherers. If I had to choose a companion for a desert island, he would be an incomparably better bet than Nicole Kidman, because he would keep the rations coming in, rain or shine.

A week or two after that desultory ratting in Suffolk, a loader in Hampshire gossiped away the day telling me about his sporting life. He reckons to shoot 150 deer a year, and disdains the game dealers to sell the carcasses.

He butchers every beast himself, taking half an hour apiece, hanging them in his own larder for a week in the skin, another week out of it. By cutting and jointing the meat and selling it direct, he gets about four times the butcher's nugatory price for venison. And he obviously takes pride in every moment of his work. Our conversation stretched to more remote reaches of sport. He loads all his own ammunition for a .243, and passionately believes that the trouble he takes is reflected in the accuracy he thus achieves. He pulls through the rifle after every shot, and zeroes his telescope meticulously before every outing.

His observations on my own shooting were laconic. 'I reckon he wasn't too bothered by that,' he chuckled after I missed a high, fast cock with both barrels. He described his own enthusiasm for rabbit-shooting with a .22: 'I can eyeball a bunny at a hundred yards,' he said with a grin, and I do not think he was boasting. He spoke with zest and reverence for pigeon-shooting – he does a lot of guiding between February and high summer, and on a good day comes home with a hundred odd. He eats the breasts as eagerly as he digests a rabbit. We discussed the finer points of game cookery, in which he takes a keen interest. I asked for his telephone number, saying that I would like to go pigeon-shooting with him some time. When we parted, however, he forgot to give it to me. I suspect this was because he did not think me enough of a shot to fancy an outing together. I was sad, but sympathetic.

My point about both the men I have sketched above is that they seem to represent the higher reaches of field sports, approached from both ends socially, if you know what I mean. Many of us spend a lot of leisure hours shooting or fishing, yet we seldom get into the dirty work: plucking and butchering, rough fishing and wild shooting. If a trout or salmon is lurking in a difficult place, we wander upstream, looking for another fish in an easier spot. If we have not been invited to a smart shoot, we do not bother to go in search of a bird or two in a wilderness. I like to think that when I was younger I was up for anything, from the days that I would bicycle five miles to shoot pigeons as a teenager. But now I have got lazy, and maybe a little spoilt as well as a little old. I do not try so hard. Talking to those two sportsmen made me feel guilty, because I wondered whether I am losing touch with the very things that justify any of us in pursuing game: a willingness for exertion, a taste for a little risk, for trying to do things that are hard, that do not include standing on a peg all day while birds are driven over our lazy heads.

That fine writer T.H. White wrote seventy years ago that sport is only sport when it is difficult. It becomes a thing of beauty only when we succeed in making a shot or a cast against the odds. I do not think he would have included in this definition hitting a stratospheric Devon pheasant with a variable-choke over-and-under gun with heavy-load cartridges, which he would have deemed a load of horse droppings. White was talking about catching a big trout by stalking it for an hour and flicking a fly under a low overhanging branch, or shooting a snipe in an Irish bog with a leg caught in a fence and one's whole body waterlogged after falling in the last morass. Effort,

together with triumph against discomfort and circumstances, make up great sporting moments. They come
only to those who search them out, who do not confine
themselves to casting down the fast water of famous pools,
or who frequent only great shoots on great days.

One day a year or so ago, I took the first sportsman I
mentioned out on our local chalk stream. Conditions were
poor. We had not accomplished much when I retired
home to work, leaving him to fish alone. When I phoned
later to see how he had got on, he described with joy but
without vanity how he had somehow stumbled into one
five-pounder in the heavy water below a sluice gate, and
another in flat water a little higher, where nobody usually
bothers to fish.

I do not think my second case-study bothers much with
fishing, but his glee in describing dropping a roe during
a few seconds' exposure on a ride at a summer dawn is
of the same persuasion. Meeting these men and hearing
their tales stirred my imagination, challenged my fancy.
If I wish to continue to think myself a real hunter, I
thought, I must try harder. I must consciously seek out
more difficult quarry. If it is easy, it ain't sport.

30

Places we Know

$\mathcal{F}$OR MOST OF us, a significant part of the joy of sport stems from practising it in places where we feel at ease, which is not often the case on a first visit. Although it is great fun to encounter a new river or a new shoot, the richest pleasures come from seeing the same drives or pools year after year. Hence, I am a little bemused by 'flying syndicates', which choose to ring the changes every time their members pick up guns. On such terms, it is hard to get to know any tract of country well enough to love it.

It is so rewarding to develop an intimate acquaintance with coverts, to know what various winds will do to the birds, to look out for the old cock slipping back, to be able to anticipate that there will be a flush on the south side just before the end. A shooting day in a familiar setting becomes even better if we meet the same fellow-guns from year to year. This helps one to relax, because one has given up hoping to impress them. It can be exhausting, getting on terms with six or seven new faces in a day. Even seeing old foes, if one has been sparring with them for long enough, can be more rewarding than meeting a host of strangers. The nicest sporting days I had last year were not the biggest – indeed, were sometimes among the smallest. They were simply the outings spent among people one knew and loved.

Continuity counts for much in everything associated with the countryside, from year to year or century to century. This is why we feel so embittered by the Labour government's efforts to destroy it. Almost anyone who belongs to a rural community, especially a landowner, recognises the need to think long, to acknowledge the value of sustained relationships, whether with employees, neighbours, fellow-sportsmen or the land and waters themselves. It is twice as much fun to fish a river beside a gillie with whom one has cast a fly for many seasons. It is usually possible to pick up a conversation exactly where one abandoned it amid the same current 358 days earlier. For some years I visited a shoot in Wiltshire which has now been broken up. Today, driving past its woods, I feel a stab of regret not only for the place, which showed splendid birds, but also for the company of the keeper, by common consent one of the nicest men in the county.

Occasionally, of course, continuity becomes mindless and obsessive. Some elderly keepers go on doing the same drive in the same way season after season, apparently oblivious of the fact that its 'young' trees have now grown thirty feet higher, or that a contrary wind is bound to turn every bird in the place. Most of us, however, have cause to be grateful for an addiction to custom, which causes hosts to go on inviting the same people to shoot, even when they must have noticed that some of us can do no more justice to their tall pheasants than George W. Bush to Osama bin Laden. Each summer one waits in suspense to see whether this is the year one gets dropped off the list for High Moor, or whatever the place is called. Having attained a certain age, I become conscious that there are only a finite number of shoots left in Britain which have not yet discovered my limitations both as guest and marksman.

On the other side of the coin, every guest knows a few places he will be happy never to see again. I am thinking of a famous West Country shoot, which boasts one of the cockiest and most notoriously obnoxious keepers in the land. He shouts instructions and reproaches at guns during drives, flatters the grand in a fashion one of Caligula's courtiers would have envied, and struts across the countryside with all the confidence of a man with a cushy billet and a giant ego. However splendid his birds, I would rather course cockroaches than go back to that estate.

We all have memories of the odd sporting day at which the social life seemed to compare unfavourably with that on offer at an undertakers' convention. Some people seem determined to carry a cargo of gloom or aggression even on a brilliant frosty November morning in the stubble. In my case, though I am sure not in yours, there are also places where one has misbehaved or blundered. I am haunted by recollection of a Scottish forest where some years ago, without excuse, at a range of a hundred yards, I wounded a stag. We caught up with it in the end, but I felt so ashamed of my own performance that I would rather not look that stalker in the eye again.

Despite my remarks above about the joy of shooting in

the same company from season to season, there are several moors where I hope devoutly not to be allotted the same loader as last time, because he is sure to remember the drive where I killed six grouse for forty cartridges. In my younger days, I was prone to lament the severance of a relationship with a river or shoot I had grown familiar with. There was a house in the north of Sutherland which meant everything to me in my twenties, and a little shoot in Northamptonshire which I ran for a decade. At both I touched pinnacles of laughter and happiness, as well as doing all manner of silly things.

For a year or two after my connection with them ended, I sighed for lost pleasures. Yet nowadays, one perceives that everything has its time and its passing. As one window closes, another opens. The great thing is to enjoy these idylls while they are there, then to find new ones to replace them as life moves on, circumstances change. I declined a kind invitation a season or two ago to return to a shoot I used to know well, and indeed to love, in the Midlands. I cherish the memories, but revisiting them would stir ghosts. Nowadays, I am content to have forged other links with other places, which I hope will prove as long-lasting and rewarding as those of the past.

31

Pigeons in the Offing

I<small>T</small> <small>SAYS</small> <small>A</small> lot about modern shooting in the south of England that if you start talking about a really cracking day which costs less than a weekend in Paris, many people will think that either you are a professional poacher or you can't add up. Then mention pigeon, and snobs say that you are cheating. Yet many of us, including me, got our shooting start in life on pigeon. For years I have been wanting to renew acquaintance with the sport, alongside my children. But it is no longer easy, if it is even possible, simply to ring up a local farmer and ask if you can go and spend an afternoon on his peas. He has regulars, just as he does for pheasants and partridges. The pressure on every kind of shooting has become over-whelming.

That is where professional pigeon guides like Richard Lovell come in. Richard arranges days wherever birds happen to be feeding over a large tract of Wiltshire and Dorset. His fees allow you to take your boys on a first-class day without a financial qualm. Even the experts cannot promise to deliver big numbers of pigeon to order. But, given a fair wind and a bit of luck, the countless hours Lovell spends spying pigeon and watching their favourite spots pay off when he takes you out. Having passed a glorious afternoon on a Dorset rape stubble with Richard and my son Harry, I was reminded that when pigeon-shooting works, it offers some of the most marvellous fun in the countryside.

Richard placed a companion named Jamie Lee in my hide on the edge of the rape stubble to keep me company. He reckons Jamie is the best pigeon shot in the country. Jamie started proving it when I missed the first three birds that dropped in, and he dropped them dead after I sat down. 'Just remember you've almost always got a lot of time with pigeon,' he said. 'You don't have to hurry it.' He cheered me up by remarking that Dylan Williams of the Royal Berkshire Shooting School, a terrific shot, had been out with them not long ago. Dylan, too, found hitting pigeon pretty hard. It is a vastly different discipline from shooting driven birds, and in many ways a more testing one. Those wily grey nomads offer every kind of shot, and few of them are easy.

The clouds were coasting slowly across an almost windless blue sky. Richard was roaming about, keeping the pigeon moving. I became absorbed in peering through the camouflage netting to spot birds. I dropped a couple passing overhead, the sort of shot I am accustomed to, and began to concentrate on making better practice at meeting birds a second or two before they settled among the decoys. All afternoon they were coming singly and in pairs. 'It's the winter when you get the flocks,' said Jamie. He was still killing two for every bird I shot, but I began to fare better as I learned to time their descents.

Jamie runs a business, but seems to do nothing else but shoot, shoot, shoot – and fish a bit. Grouse, pheasants, partridges, doves, salmon, trout, pigeon are his daily fare. He goes out with Richard perhaps thirty days a year, because he knows he will meet better sport than he could find on his own: 'You tend to get the big bags in the spring, when they're drilling peas, for instance. But it's all nonsense about going for three or four hundred. We reckon fifty is a really nice day.' Richard came and stood behind us in the hide, spotting birds and talking about the vital importance of keeping farmers happy. The trouble about having Richard spectating was that, as the pigeon came in, I started missing everything – and so did Jamie. 'Never seen him shoot like this,' muttered Richard. 'Go away, Lovell,' we both said. He went off to inspect Harry, whom we could hear having the time of his life a field away. Thereafter, thank heaven, we started killing them again. 'I'm not usually too bad at shooting under pressure,' said Jamie, 'but it's tough when you can feel Richard willing one to hit the damn things.'

We had started with a dozen decoys and a wobbler on

a stake. Richard refused to use his Pigeon Magnet, the electric whirler which turns a couple of decoy birds in the air. He doesn't like to put it out unless all else fails, and that afternoon we were having plenty of sport anyway. We were getting a shot every two or three minutes.

Every half-hour or so, Jamie said: 'I'll just have a tidy up.' He ran out to check that no dead birds were lying on their backs, which puts off everything in sight, and to rearrange our decoy flock, nudging fifty strong by now.

In winter, of course, decoying is a much harsher occupation, but on that summer afternoon it seemed luxurious, sipping coffee from a well-filled lunch hamper, gossiping about sport and all the time scanning the sky intently, taking it in turns to shoot. I trimmed the tails of a few swinging fast on the right – how seldom any missing shot is ahead of the target. Not every pigeon dropped to the decoys. We saw our share of wary passers-by who took a look, disliked something they saw, and flew on high across the sky. The Hastingses had to leave after three hours. Harry had dropped a dozen for a prodigious number of cartridges. Jamie and I accounted for north of fifty, mostly his of course. He was planning on another hour or two in the hide before setting off to go bass-fishing in Poole Harbour. I felt exhausted just thinking of it.

Richard goes out maybe sixty days a year. The rest of the time he is spying in vain, the weather is wrong, or he is at his proper job on a Wiltshire estate. 'You can never be sure with pigeons, can you?' he said. 'One day they're feeding somewhere, then they've moved off. The only way you can get the sport is to keep doing what I do – driving round the countryside looking at them.' Now that traditional rough shooting has become so hard to come by, I can think of nothing better than an afternoon with Richard Lovell, especially with a boy or two in tow. The excitement of watching a bird set its wings and drop to the decoy, and the snatched shot – yes, I know Jamie was right, but I found it hard to break the habit of a lifetime – matched the beauty of the golden fields and lush trees of the English countryside looking at its best. No sportsman but a fool despises pigeon.

32

Marauders do it in the Rough

$\mathcal{O}$NCE UPON A time, January was for cocks-only days. Fifty pheasants was thought a good bag at the tail end of the season. Nowadays, I am amazed by the number of places where they continue to shoot three-figure numbers right up to the first of February. My own favourite pastime in the back-end days is to take a hand in what some hosts menacingly describe as a 'maraud'. I had never heard the term until one day in the eighties when a delightful retired Guards veteran rang from Bedfordshire, somewhat apologetically, to invite me to a day in late January: 'It'll only be a maraud, I'm afraid,' he said. 'But we'll have a wander round and see what we can find.' I turned up with a belt of cartridges, and received a game card afterwards showing that we had shot more than two hundred pheasants. This seemed a pretty grand sort of maraud.

The theory behind these enterprises, great or small, is that beaters and guns mop up odd corners that have been missed on the big days. The problem is that any bird which has survived to the last gasp of the season tends to possess the cunning of Odysseus, and is disinclined to surrender on the last lap. I took part in a couple of very jolly marauds in the back-end days last year. The first was in Norfolk. The wind was howling across the East Anglian plain, leaving no doubt that it had arrived non-stop from Siberia. 'We're going to have a look round the hedges. Lots of walking,' said our host cheerfully. A fellow-guest muttered to me: 'This is all your bloody fault for writing so many silly pieces about how much you like rough shooting.'

So I do, and so I did on that drizzly and counter-zephyrous day. Our host is an enthusiast who brings to the art of marshalling pheasants a taste for stratagem that would excite the respect of Napoleon. Beaters marched across great tracts of Norfolk, spanning about twenty acres a drive. The guns were cunningly placed to right and left and behind, to anticipate the birds' wiles, with scarcely a gun ahead of the beaters. Those pheasants which had not attended Staff College simply flew straight forward and escaped. There were, however, some sophisticated cocktail-party birds, of exactly the kind our host was looking for, which soared sideways across the wind and provided those lucky enough to be underneath them with wonderfully testing shooting. A few unsporting cocks tried to deflect destiny by slipping away knee-high, but on marauding days those get shot too.

A bonus on these occasions is that dogs are allowed to roam out of control. It is such a relief to give one's own beast licence to misbehave, when everybody else's is doing likewise. I simply hoped that Paddy would recover his manners again before discipline was reintroduced the following August. That Norfolk afternoon became a dash from drive to drive, in the hope of scouring every yard of the estate for recalcitrant pheasants before nightfall. We were carried home exhausted in twilight, with 120-odd in the bag and that most contented of all sensations, a knowledge that we had sweated for our sport.

A month later, on the last day of January, I was marauding again, in a gale in west Wiltshire. Our host is another enthusiastic strategist. The beaters were sweeping huge tracts of woodland around a deep valley. The guns were placed to surround the pheasants, who were expected to realise they had no choice save to come out with their hands up. Clausewitz would have been impressed. There was a serious mismatch, however, between the breadth of the front we were seeking to cover and the number of guns, posted at hundred-yard intervals. We could hear those pheasants laughing at us as they swung away on the wind, well missed from both flanks.

On such days, when expectations are modest and no one feels too serious, we relax. There is none of the tension of the big occasion when much is expected of guns, keeper, beaters and birds. I mused on the mossy tree-stumps, contemplated the catkins and early snowdrops and badger setts as I plunged through undergrowth behind the beaters. I took an occasional long shot at birds glimpsed for seconds between overhead branches. Paddy did a couple of good retrieves, which delighted his owner and caused any amount of tail-wagging and sighs of delight from the retriever himself. Not for nothing do we call the old dog the heavy breather.

'The pheasants were too clever for us there,' said our host as we drank whisky mac after a terrific plunge along one steep, densely wooded hillside. 'They all crept out at the top.' 'And at the bottom,' interjected a mother who had been looking on with a brace of babies. 'About ten went past six feet from my ear.' It is ever so on these expeditions. At the first drive after lunch three terrific pheasants streaked high over my head. I hit one and was ecstatic. We trudged across more miles of woody Wiltshire. The beaters hallooed boisterously each time a bird got up. A pack of spaniels coursed every pheasant that fell, with an accompanying chorus that would have made Quorn hounds envious.

Our host is well into his sixties, but he kept us marching through a vast wood until darkness had all but overtaken the party. A gale was whirling every flushed pheasant high into the sky thirty yards out of shot, pursued by a barrage of optimistic gunfire. Paddy had abandoned hunting and was trotting beside me, a sure sign of exhaustion. I was glad he did not know that this was our final chance of the season. Dogs live in perpetual hope of good things to come. On that grey January evening, I felt a pang of sorrow for the knowledge that my companion was getting old. The shooting years were drawing to an end for Paddy. He covered the ground as eagerly as ever, but one could sense him feeling his joints at every step.

Night was coming on. The beaters furled the plastic flags. I said to a neighbouring gun: 'By this time of year you feel you've had enough, don't you?' He said: 'I do for about a fortnight. Then I just want to get the bloody summer over, and start again.' Our maraud accounted for thirty-odd pheasants, my only rabbit of the season, and a prodigious number of cartridges. I locked up my gun. Anyone for tennis?

Index

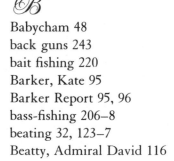